The

of Disease

Teachings on Specific Diseases and How to be Free

When In Doubt, Cast It Out

By: Jessica Jones

978-1492776024

DEDICATION

Dedicated to dear friends who have become instant family of like mind, passion and faithfulness in Yahovah.

Jessica Jones

CONTENTS

PUBLISHERS NOTES
Disclaimer

This publication is intended to provide helpful and informative material. It is not intended to diagnose, treat, cure, or prevent any health problem or condition, nor is intended to replace the advice of a physician.

Paperback Edition

Manufactured in the United States of America

Spiritual Roots of Disease

By Jessica Jones

Published by

Quiddity Press & Productions

The Spiritual Roots of Common Diseases

First Printing 2013.

Second Printing 2016.

Printed in the United States of America

Quiddity Press & Productions

Publisher's Cataloging-In-Publication
(Provided by Quiddity Press & Publications)
Jones, Jessica. – 1st ed.
Jones, Jessica. – 2nd ed.

Please do not copy and distribute this book or any part of this book. Help support the author and her efforts to bring the truth of YAHOVAH to HIS people.

Check out the end of the book for more books available by Jessica Jones.

Jessica Jones

CHAPTER 1 – INTRODUCTION

Disease is part of the curse upon man. Disease is the curse of disobedience to Torah, the inspired written Word of Yahovah. The words of Yahshua, our Messiah did not contradict, eradicate, change or eliminate the written Word of Torah, He came to clarify the mistruths of the Scribes and Pharisees. They added much confusion to the simple Word of Torah.

After the Scribes, Pharisees and Rabbis added to the Torah, the Catholic Church proceeded to take away from the Word of Torah. Deuteronomy 12:32 expressly forbids this. Every religion on earth has done this very thing. They have brought a curse upon themselves and laid that burden upon the people that follow their false teachings.

To be free from the curse of disease, poverty and death, we must repent and return to the Word of Life, the Torah in its completeness, and not just in excerpts taken to misprove points of philosophy.

Deuteronomy 28 clearly says that if we listen AND OBEY the words of Torah we will be blessed. But if we do not, we will be cursed.

Deuteronomy 28:1, 2 If you listen closely to what ADONAI your God says, observing and obeying all his mitzvot which I am giving you today, ADONAI your God will raise you high above all the nations on earth; and all the following blessings will be yours in abundance -if you will do what ADONAI your God says

List of the Blessings:

- A blessing on you in the city
- A blessing on you in the countryside
- A blessing on the fruit of your body, the fruit of your land and the fruit of your livestock
- A blessing on your grain-basket and kneading-bowl
- A blessing on you when you go out, and a blessing on you when you come in
- ADONAI will cause your enemies attacking you to be defeated before you; they will advance on you one way and flee before you seven ways
- ADONAI will order a blessing to be with you in your barns and in everything you undertake
- ADONAI will bless you in the land ADONAI your God is giving you
- ADONAI will establish you as a people separated out for himself, as he has sworn to you - if you will observe the mitzvot of ADONAI your God and follow his ways, then all the peoples on earth will see that ADONAI's name, his presence, is with you; so that they will be afraid of you.
- ADONAI will give you great abundance of good things - of the fruit of your body, the fruit of your livestock and the fruit of your land in the land ADONAI swore to your ancestors to give you.
- ADONAI will open for you his good treasure, the sky, to give your land its rain at the right seasons and to bless everything you undertake. You will lend to many nations and not borrow

- ADONAI will make you the head and not the tail; and you will be only above, never below - if you will listen to, observe and obey the mitzvot of ADONAI your God

Deuteronomy 28:14, 15 But if you refuse to pay attention to what ADONAI your God says, and do not observe and obey all his mitzvot and regulations which I am giving you today, then all the following curses will be yours in abundance:

- A curse on you in the city, and a curse on you in the countryside
- A curse on your grain-basket and kneading-bowl
- A curse on the fruit of your body, the fruit of your land and the young of your cattle and flocks
- A curse on you when you come in, and a curse on you when you go out.
- ADONAI will send on you curses, disasters and frustration in everything you set out to do, until you are destroyed and quickly perish, because of your evil actions in abandoning me
- ADONAI will bring on you a plague that will stay with you until he has exterminated you from the land you are entering in order to take possession of it.
- ADONAI will strike you down with wasting diseases, fever, inflammation, fiery heat, drought, blasting winds and mildew; and they will pursue you until you perish.
- The sky over your head will be brass and the earth under you iron. ADONAI will turn the rain your

land needs into powder and dust that will fall on you from the sky until you are destroyed.

- ADONAI your God will cause you to be defeated before your enemies; you will advance on them one way and flee before them seven.
- You will become an object of horror to every kingdom on earth. Your carcasses will become food for all the birds in the air and the wild animals, and there will be no one to scare them away.
- ADONAI will strike you down with the boils that broke out on the Egyptians, tumors, skin lesions and itching, all incurable.
- ADONAI will strike you with insanity, blindness and utter confusion. You will grope about at noon like a blind person groping in the dark, unable to find your way.
- You will be continually oppressed and robbed, and there will be no one to save you.
- You will get engaged to a woman, but another man will marry her.
- You will build a house but not live in it.
- You will plant a vineyard but not use its fruit.
- Your ox will be slaughtered before your eyes, but you won't eat any of its meat.
- Your donkey will be taken away from you by force as you watch, and you won't get it back.
- Your sheep will be given to your enemies, and there will be no one to help you.
- Your sons and daughters will be handed over to another people; you will watch for them longingly

all day but not see them; and there will be nothing you can do about it.

- A nation unknown to you will eat the fruit of your land and labor.
- Yes, you will be continually oppressed and crushed, till you go crazy from what your eyes have to see.
- ADONAI will strike you down in the knees and legs with painful and incurable boils; they will spread from the sole of your foot to the crown of your head.
- ADONAI will bring you and your king whom you have put over yourselves to a nation you have not known, neither you nor your ancestors; and there you will serve other gods made of wood and stone.
- You will be so devastated as to become a proverb and a laughingstock among all the peoples to which ADONAI will drive you.
- You will carry much seed out to the field but gather little in, because locusts will devour it.
- You will plant vineyards and dress them but neither drink the wine nor gather the grapes, because worms will eat them.
- You will have olive trees throughout your territory but not anoint yourself with the oil, because your olives will fall off unripe.
- You will father sons and daughters, but they won't belong to you, because they will go into captivity.
- The bugs will inherit all your trees and the produce of your land.
- The foreigner living with you will rise higher and higher while you sink lower and lower. He will lend

to you, but you will not lend to him; he will be the head and you the tail.

Deuteronomy 28:45-47 All these curses will come on you, pursuing you and overtaking you until you are destroyed, because you didn't pay attention to what ADONAI your God said, observing his mitzvot and regulations that he gave you. These curses will be on you and your descendants as a sign and a wonder forever. Because you didn't serve ADONAI your God with joy and gladness in your heart when you had such an abundance of everything;

Our current condition is because of generational disobedience to Torah, the Word and Law of Yahovah.

For centuries the Catholic church has taught that once saved, we are perfectly cleansed, pure and righteous immediately after we accept Yahshua into our lives.

Paul tells us in Romans 7 and 8 that we do the things we don't want to do, and don't do the things we want to do because **the man of sin dwells within us**. HE WAS SPEAKING TO THE CHURCH.

To teach that Christians cannot be possessed is false. It is deception, wrongly taught by pastors and teachers out of stubborn ignorance. They keep their people in bondage for lack of searching out the truth. "My people perish for lack of knowledge" says Yahovah.

We forget or ignore that Yahshua did three things.

- First, He first taught the truth, exposing that which was added to the Word by the Scribes and Pharisees.

- Second, He came to deliver His people who learned and embraced the truth.

- Lastly, He came to heal the people who embraced both teaching and deliverance.

This is the three-fold prescription for healing – accepting truth, embracing deliverance and allowing healing/blessing to overtake us. There is no other way.

Yahshua came to teach the truth without all the embellishments and by showing His people, the chosen people, the Hebrews that despite their overboard piety, they were possessed. He came to pay the price of our sin with His own sinless life. And He came to bring life by his words so that we could be taught, delivered, healed and set free.

But that is not what we do today. We make it into a show and tell. We make it into a mysterious, frightening process instead of realizing the truth and simplicity of it.

Eve and Adam sinned. This allowed HaSatan entrance into our natural, universal realm. HaSatan ruled and reined over our lives for 1,000 miserable years before the flood. In that time over 7 billion people perished in the flood for lack of truth.

Since then, the lifespan of man has been reduced to slow down the progression of sin. But in the following 3,000 years, Nimrod, Semiramus and Tammuz raised the false religion of Cain once again. It continues to rain down destruction. These are people who knew the truth. They had, at one time, embraced the truth. But they reverted back into perversion of that truth once again.

As punishment, mankind was dispersed to the horizons speaking different languages, each one embracing a different version of the heresy taught by Nimrod.

False religions multiplied as the nations spread ever outward from the Middle East. And their manufactured gods and customs travelled with them. Each single band of peoples tweaked their beliefs just a little, but they were still based on the same twist on truth.

Every lie embraced, trauma experienced and unrepentant sin was another door opened for yet another spirit to enter in, further deceiving the people. Eventually, like the man from Gadarenes, we are a people possessed by both current and generational spirits embedded within us. And like Paul, we do the things we don't want to do and don't do the things we want to do...because of this demonic influence.

Pastors and religious leaders who ignore this reality teach the people to curse themselves with their sin and passions. Their responsibility is to show the way of escape provided by Yahovah Himself. Repentance and salvation by the sacrificed blood of the only innocent man to ever live, Yahshua is the way of blessing. Read how Balaam did this very thing to his own people, for money.

Jessica Jones

We accept Yahshua as our Lord and Savior, presumably repenting for personal and generational sins, but then allow the spirits that have possessed us and our family line for generations to remain. They are still within us. We are to work out our salvation with fear and trembling *daily. The Holy Spirit shows us the things that remain within us.* Go back to our Father Yahovah and repent of what Ruach HaKodesh (Holy Spirit) has shown. Deliverance is a working out our salvation step by step as He reveals to us what needs to be repented of AND removed from our lives.

Accepting Yahshua as our Messiah gives us the authority to repent and cast out these spirits that have taken up residence within us. We need to send them to the pit where they belong. Do not allow them to remain on the earth. We are given authority through Yahshua to restore the Garden relationship. It is by Yahshua's sacrifice that we have this authority and ability. It is by Yahshua's sacrifice that we can begin to be free and it is by Ruach HaKodesh's comfort and guidance that we can regain this freedom. It is not an immediate deliverance but a gradual deliverance as we remove mind-sets, spirits, habits, inappropriate personality traits, etc. until we become like our Messiah and Father, not through our own works, but through the work of His sacrifice.

In this work you will find an extensive compilation of many of the things that afflict us. Throughout the years that I have used these guidelines, many including myself have been released from much affliction. Prayer and the guidance of Holy Spirit will lead you where you need to go.

Yahovah bless you in your struggle to become more like Him and free from the bondage of HaSatan.

CHAPTER 2 – IN WHOSE NAME DO WE PRAY?

When praying, remember YOU HAVE THE AUTHORITY ONLY THROUGH THE SACRIFICE OF YAHSHUA. It is not yours to wield in arrogance but neither is it to be wielded with fear.

There are those who would teach we cannot do it ourselves, we need to pay $1,000 to have some ministry deliver us.

That was the purpose of Yahshua's sacrifice. He died to pay the price of our sin. He suffered and died to reclaim the ownership of the natural universe that Adam handed over to HaSatan. He rose, Lord and King, as the first fruits of our own rising above our sin and death into life.

Lucifer and his demons tremble at the limited time before they face the Lake of Fire, their fate already sealed by their own unrepentant hatred. Their fate is already sealed. Our fate is not, despite their lie to the contrary.

There is but one requirement to see eternity. Honesty. Our own naked honesty.

We need to acknowledge that we have sinned, that is, to have missed the mark that sets the bar. We have missed the mark set by our Creator, whose nature is love. We have sinned by putting ourselves first. We put our own pleasures first, our own desires first before that of others.

We have sinned because we lie about our own nature. We try to hide our sin under cover of secrecy.

We need to acknowledge that it was our sin that made it necessary for the Son of Yahovah, Yahshua the Messiah, to give His life to pay the price for our guilt. There is no other name or sacrifice by which freedom and life will come. There is only one name and it is not the name of the Pope, the Preacher, Allah, Jesus, Buddha or anything else. The only name that can save is Yahshua, the Messiah Son of Yahovah. Jesus is the name given by the Catholics, a variation of the spelling of Iesous, which means, Hail (Ie) Zeus (Sous). The letter "J" did not come into any language until 1700AD.

There is only one name under heaven that will save us and that is the name of the Son of Yahovah, Yahshua. Not Zeus, Helios, Allah, Buddha or even Tammuz, all of whom are also known as Jesus.

> "The name Jesus is NOT a derivative of YHWH (Jehovah). There is great cause for alarm when this hybrid Greek name is being plied into Messiah because not only is it NOT the sanctified given name of Yeshua (Yahoshua) but prophetic and sanctified unity within the Word of YHWH is lost! Early Christo-Pagans syncretized Greek culture into Greek Christianity, which "smoothed" the way for Christo-Paganism to become the "state" religion." - Is the name "Jesus" holy? *Baruch Ben Daniel*

> "They (the Graeco-Roman World) had worshipped Zeus as the supreme deity. Their savior was Zeus,

so now they were ready to accept Jehoshua as Jesus - Iesous, meaning - hail Zeus. Now our translated scriptures say that Jahwah's (Jehovah's) Son's name is Jesus, which is a compound word made up of Ie and Zeus (Hail Zeus)." *-The Origin of Christianity by A.B. Traina*

"This name of the true Messiah, Jahshuwah (Jehoshua), being Hebrew, was objectionable to the Greeks and Romans, who hated the Judeans (Jews), and so it was deleted from the records, and a new name inserted. Jahshuwah (Jehoshua) was thus replaced by Ie-Sous (hail Zeus), now known to us as Jesus." *-The Origin of Christianity by A.B. Traina*

In one hundred short years after Yahshua and His Apostles were removed through death, Constantine took over the Truth and Faith and attempted to mold and conform it into the image of his sun god worship. He worshipped Helios and Zeus and through the symbol of the cross, he was directed in vision to take over the world.

He did so by taking over the faith of the Messiah by combining some truth with his pagan faith and traditions. He has conquered the world inch by inch. His kingdom has lasted for almost 2,000 years. We know it as the Roman Catholic Church.

It is not through the name of the Roman god Jesus that we are saved but through the name of the Messiah, Son of Yahovah we are saved. And that name is Yahshua.

So it is in the name of Yahovah and Yahshua that I pray.

CHAPTER 3 – THE PRAYER

Remember, be honest.

There are many things to remember in your honesty. I will guide you through them.

First, there are NO secret sins.

If there were 7 billion people in the earth when the flood came and there are currently over 7 billion people in the earth after 6,000 years of birth and death, how many angels do you think there were?

We are such a small minded people. We forget that Yahovah is a mighty God, Creator of ALL THINGS. And He does not think small.

There were trillions of angels created. I cannot conceive of the number of them. In fact, there might even be more than that – the largest number known to man is *googleplex* and there just might be a googleplex of angels. If Abraham descendants were to be more numerous than the sands of the sea, why would Yahovah create the number of angels that could be counted by man?

There are more angels than we will ever know. And one-third of them fell.

Since the man of Gadarenes had over 1,000 demons in him at the time of his deliverance by Yahshua and there are 7 billion people in the earth today, that means there are well over 7,000,000,000,000 demons in the earth. But, this is a very conservative number.

Think about this. Regardless what you do, sleeping, eating, walking, driving, talking, stealing, looking at someone in lust, fornicating, committing adultery, gossiping about someone, slander, lying, cursing, getting drunk...whatever, you are surrounded by demons watching. You do nothing in secret. Your life is an open book to an invisible world of angels, demons and Yahovah Himself.

When you cry from an emotional wound and trauma, there is an angel there that gathers your tears in a vial to be stored for judgment day. This is because the cause of the shed tear is stored in the tear and will be shown for viewing and testimony on the Day of Judgment.

Everything we think, say and do is recorded for evidence on Judgment Day, either for or against us. There is NO HIDDEN SIN NOW OR EVER. All will be revealed. All is known.

So we need only be honest about every sin. And since sin is *missing the mark*, what mark is being missed? It is the mark found in Torah.

Exodus20:6 – Yahovah shows mercy to those who OBEY HIS COMMANDMENTS.

Deuteronomy 4:2 – We are not to ADD to the Word of Torah as the Jews, nor are we to SUBTRACT from the Word of Torah as the Catholics, Protestants and Christian religions, so that we may keep the commandments of Yahovah.

Deuteronomy 10:13 – the Commandments of Yahovah are for our good and not our death or harm.

Nehemiah 1:5 – to show that we love Yahovah, we will keep His commandments.

John 14:15 – Yahshua tells us that if we love Him we will keep His commandments.

John 14:21 – Yahshua tells us that ONLY those who have the commandments of Yahovah AND keep them, are those who love Him.

John 15:10 – Yahshua tells us that only by keeping His commandments are we in His love.

1 John 5:2 – We can only truly love the children of Yahovah by loving Yahovah AND keeping His commandments.

1 John 5:3 – It is the love of Yahovah that we keep His commandments and do not find them grievous.

Revelation 14:12 – The patience of the saints is two-fold. They are seen and known by keeping the commandments of Yahovah and have accepted and have faith in the Messiah, Yahshua.

The commandments of Yahovah are the mark we are to hit. They are His nature. They are His love. They are our protection against the evils of this world and evils of the spiritual world.

The truth of spirit assignments is this.

> **Revelation 2:14** Nevertheless, I have a few things against you: you have some people who hold to the teaching of Bil'am, who taught Balak to **set a trap for the people** of Isra'el, **so that they would eat food that had been sacrificed to idols and commit sexual sin**.

This is what spirits do. They enter into us through a trauma, shock, pain, etc. They do this because these strong sudden emotions open a door into us. Then they teach us to *miss the mark* of the commandments of Yahovah by causing us to eat food sacrificed to idols and commit sexual sin. They teach us to ignore the Word of Yahovah, ignore His commandments including His Feast Days and keep every tradition, practice and ceremony of pagan origin.

"Well, Jesus is the reason for the season."

Very true. He is. Yahshua is not the reason for the season, but Zeus or Helios, the Sun god is the reason for the season. Tammuz is the reason for the season as instituted by Semiramus. The *season* is bathed in blood, sorrow, tears and human sacrifice.

"Well, Jesus knows my heart and that I think of him during Christmas."

Again, very true. Jesus does know your heart because Jesus, in truth, with the mask ripped off, is Lucifer. He knows his spies are in you to teach you to curse yourself so that you will reap the harvest of curses in Deuteronomy 28 and not the blessings.

Keeping pagan holidays, eating unclean foods, believing things that have been ADDED to Torah/Tanakh and committing sexual sins are all missing the mark, are all sin and bring on the curse of disease, spiritual and financial destruction, with the final outcome being death in the Lake of Fire.

Do not deceive yourself or lull yourself into the false teaching that – Jesus knows my heart and will forgive me. Jesus is NOT the Son of Yahovah, our Creator, but Zeus/Helios/Tammuz better known as Lucifer or Satan, the Father of Lies.

Yahshua is the Son of Yahovah, our Creator. Yahshua will only forgive those things we honestly confess and put under the sacrifice of His shed blood. Once done, it is removed from the record of the books in heaven and the memory of Yahovah Himself.

So be honest. Line yourself up with Torah. Confess those things you have failed in. Repent and put them under the blood of Yahshua. Ask for forgiveness, embrace His forgiveness and freedom.

In the following chapters I have included a list of diseases. This is your starting point. Do you have physical problems, illness and diseases in your life? If so, search out the disease and discover what is behind that affliction. Behind each disease name you will find the list of *spirits.* Repent and remove each one. Ask Ruach HaKodesh if there are others.

Remember, there are NO secret sins. All is recorded. So you have nothing to lose by being honest except the sin itself.

Confess the sin and cast out the spirit to the pit where it belongs. Then embrace the healing from freedom as your body lines up with the blessings of Yahovah and removes itself from the curses of breaking Torah.

But remember, learn what the standard is, so that you will not miss the mark in the future. Step out from the teachings of Balaam – the current teachings of all world religions such as Catholicism, Protestantism, Judaism, Islam, Buddha, and the 40,000+ other religions smothering the world today.

This is what Yahshua taught. He taught the people, delivered the people and then healed the people. Embrace His way. The Truth.

PRAYER:

Father Yahovah, I repent, renounce and fall out of agreement with the spirits of (name spirits by name) both generationally and current in my life. I place my confessed sins under the blood of Yahshua, to be forever covered, removed and paid for. By the shed blood of the Messiah, Yahshua, I break the power of (name the spirits by name) and cancel their assignment in my life and I cast them to the pit in the name of Yahovah. Ruach HaKodesh, I ask that you rise up and fill the areas that were occupied by these spirits and heal me. I speak peace and rest to my body, soul and spirit in the name of Yahovah. Amen.

Father Yahovah, I break the power of every word, thought, deed, curse, promise, dedication and vow spoken against me or my family line throughout the generations. I break their power and cancel their assignment on my life and command them now, in the name of Yahovah, to fall to the ground null and void. By the blood of Yahshua, I speak blessing where there was curse, freedom where there was bondage, restoration of my DNA throughout the bloodline to liberate me from these curses. By the shed blood of the Messiah, Yahshua, I break the power of the (name the curse) and cancel their assignment in my life in the name of Yahovah. Ruach HaKodesh, I ask that you rise up and fill the areas that were occupied by these spirits and heal me. I speak peace and restoration to my body, soul and spirit in the name of Yahovah. Amen.

CHAPTER 4 – 12 FORBIDDEN HEATHEN PRACTICES

There is absolutely nothing righteous, good, acceptable or remotely redeemable about anything occultic. These teachings, lies, misconceptions and practices come from Lucifer himself as a counterfeit of truth. They have one end – death.

Those who follow Yahshua cannot go to fortune tellers, listen to New Age teachings or accept soothsaying practices in the name of *Jesus*.

Today, not only the obvious occultic teachings abound, but we are buried in "Christian Magick" as well. So many church leaders practice the art of sorcery, witchcraft, enchantments and divination in their *prophetic teachings*. All masked in Chrisianese, of course.

So many of our traditions stem from these practices which are taken from ancient pagan ways. They are simply accepted as our heritage and national identity, regardless of what that national identity is.

In every case, these 12 Heathen practices are working with Familiar Spirits. These Familiar Spirits taught our ancestors how to stray from the truth into gross error, just as they are hard at work continuing to teach us today.

In every case, these 12 Heathen practices are not fun, amusing, interesting, curious or anything other than what they are designed to be. They bring death.

Enchantments, Magick – Ex 7:11,22, 8:7,18, Lev 19:26, Deut 18:10, 2 Chr 3:3,6, 2, 2 Ki 21:6, 2 Ki 17:17, 21:6, Isa 47:9,12, Jer 27:9, Da 1:20

The Merriam-Webster Dictionary: enchant:

- To attract and hold attention of someone by being interesting, pretty, etc.
- To influence by or as if by charms and incantation
- To attract and move deeply, rouse to ecstatic admiration
- To chant
- Synonyms: allure, beguile, bewitch, captivate, charm, fascinate, kill, magnetize, wile, witch

Be not deceived. Speak honest words and not words to entrap or illicit a certain response.

Witchcraft: Practice of Dealing with Spirits – Ex 22:18, Deut 18:10, 1 Sa 15:23, 2 Chr 33:6, 2 Ki 9:22, Mic 5:12, Nah 3:4, Gal 5:19-21

The Merriam-Webster Dictionary: witchcraft:

- The use of sorcery or magic (magick)
- Communication with the devil or with a familiar spirit
- An irresistible influence or fascination
- Synonyms: bewitchery, bewitchment, conjuring, devilry, deviltry, diablerie, enchantment, ensorcellement, mojo, necromancy, sorcery, thaumaturgy, voodooism, magic, magick, witchery, wizardry

Be not deceived. Speak honest communication with Yahovah, your Creator and not Lucifer, Familiar Spirits or even false leaders to illicit help and understanding.

Sorcery: Black and White Magick, Potion, etc. – Ex 7:11, Isa 4:9, 57:3, Jer 27:9, Da 2:2, Mal 3:5, Acts 8:9-11, 13:6-8, Rev 9:21, 18:23, 21:8, 22:15

The Merriam-Webster Dictionary: sorcery:

- The use of magical powers that are obtained through evil spirits
- The use of power gained from the assistance or control of evil spirits especially for divining
- Synonyms: bewitchery, bewitchment, conjuring, devilry, deviltry, diablerie, enchantment, ensorcellment, mojo, necromancy, magic, magick, thaumaturgy, voodooism, witchery, wizardry

Be not deceived. Speak honest words of confession and submission to He Who Created you and not words to gain power, control and prominence over another.

Soothsaying – Isa 2:6, Da 2:27, 4:7, 5:7,11, Mic 5:12

The Merriam-Webster Dictionary: soothsaying:

- The act of foretelling events
- Prediction
- Prophesy (not the true Word of Yahovah but that of our own making and calling it by His name)
- Synonyms: auguring, augury, bodement, cast, forecast, forecasting, foretelling, predicting, presaging, prognosis, prognostic, prognosticating, prognostication, prophesy, prediction, vaticination

Be not deceived. Speak honest words and not words made up to appear important and gain honor and recognition.

Divination: Art of Mystic Insight or Fortune Telling – Num 22:7, 23:23, Deut 18:10-14, 2 Ki 17:17, 1 Sa 6:2, Jer 14:14, 27:9, 29:8, Ex 12:24, 13:6-7,23, 21:22-29, 22:28, Mic 3:7, Zech 10:2, Acts 16:16

The Merriam-Webster Dictionary: foretelling:

- To describe something before it happens
- To predict
- To tell beforehand
- Synonyms: augur, call, forecast, predict, presage, prognosticate, prophesy, read, vaticinate

Be not deceived. Speak honest words and not vain imaginations of unknown events to secure fame, recognition or importance.

Wizardry – Ex 22:18, Lev 19:31, 20:6, 27, Deut 18:11, 1 Sam 28:3,9, 2 Ki 21:6, 23:24, 2 Chr 33:6, Isa 19:3

The Merriam-Webster Dictionary: wizardry/wizard:

- The magical things done by a wizard
- A seemingly magical transforming power or influence
- Great skill or cleverness in an activity
- Wizard: a person who is skilled in magic or who has magical powers
- Wizard: a sorcerer
- Wizard: a person who is a magician (who uses misdirection)

- Synonyms: charmer, conjurer, conjuror, enchanter, mage, Magian, magus, necromancer, sorcerer, voodoo, voodooist, witch, magician

Be not deceived. Speak honest words and not words of fantasy, illusion, misdirection or false powers or influence.

Necromancy: Real or Pretend Communication with the Dead – Deut 18:11, Isa 8:19, 1 Sam 28, 1 Chr 10:13

The Merriam-Webster Dictionary: necromancy:

- The practice of talking to the spirits of dead people
- The use of magic powers especially for evil purposes
- The conjuration of the spirits of the dead for purposes of magically revealing the future or influencing the course of events
- Synonyms: bewitchery, bewitchment, conjuring, devilry, deviltry, diablerie, enchantment, ensorcellment, mojo, magic, sorcery, thaumaturgy, voodooism, witchcraft, witchery, wizardry Speak honest words and not words to entrap or illicit a certain response.

Be not deceived. Speak honest words and not words that whisper into the ears of spirits and listen for the words of spirits to whisper in your ear.

Magick: Pretend or Real Supernatural Practice – Ge 41:8,24, Ex 7:11,22, 8:7,18-19, 9:11, Da 1:20, 2:2,10,27, 4:7,9, 5:11, Acts 19:19

The Merriam-Webster Dictionary: magic:

- A power that allows people, witches and wizards to do impossible things by saying special words or performing special actions
- Tricks that seem to be impossible and that are done by a performer to entertain people
- A special power, influence, or skill
- The use of means such as charms or spells believed to have supernatural power over natural forces
- Magic rites, incantations or ceremonies
- An extraordinary power or influence seemingly from a supernatural source
- Something that seems to cast a spell: enchantment
- The art of producing illusions by sleight of hand
- Synonyms: bewitchery, bewitchment, conjuring, devilry (or deviltry), diablerie, enchantment, ensorcellment, mojo, necromancy, sorcery, thaumaturgy, voodooism, witchcraft, witchery, wizardry

Be not deceived. Speak honest words and not words or deeds to trick people or for gain, control and mastery of people.

Charm: Spells, Enchanting – Deut 18:11, Isa 19:3

The Merriam-Webster Dictionary: charm:

- Something that is believed to have magic powers and specially to prevent bad luck
- A small ornament worn on a bracelet or chain
- To put a spell on someone or something
- To cause someone to like you or to do what you want by being nice, friendly, etc.
- To affect by or as if by magic: compel

- To please, soothe, or delight by compelling attraction
- To endow with or as if with supernatural powers by means of charms
- To protect by or as if by spells, charms, or supernatural influences
- To control an animal typically by charms (ex. snake charmer)
- To practice magic and enchantment
- To have the effect of a charm: fascinate
- The chanting or reciting of a magic spell: incantation
- A practice or expression believed to have magic power
- Something worn about the person to ward off evil or ensure good fortune: amulet
- A trait that fascinates, allures, or delights
- An enhanced physical grace or attraction that is compelling
- Synonyms: amulet, fetish, fetich, mascot, mojo, periapt, phylactery, talisman, allure, beguile, bewitch, captivate, enchant, fascinate, kill, magnetize, wile, witch

Be not deceived. Speak honest words and not words to entrap or force others to appreciate, admire, follow, etc. you.

Prognostication: Foretell Future by Indications, Omens, Signs, etc. – Isa 47:13

The Merriam-Webster Dictionary: prognostication:

- To give an indication in advance
- To give a foretoken

- An act, the fact, or the power of prognosticating
- To forecast
- To give a foreboding
- Synonyms: auguring, augury, bodement, cast, forecast, forecasting, foretelling, predicting, presaging, prognosis, prognostic, prognosticating, prediction, prophecy, prophesy, soothsaying, vaticination

Be not deceived. Speak honest words and fanciful words of events that have not happened in order to receive recognition, importance, or fame.

Observing Pagan Times: Other than Feasts of the Lord in Torah – Lev 19:26, Deut 18:10, 2 Ki 21:6, 2 Chr 33:6

The Merriam-Webster Dictionary: pagan:

- Heathen follower of a polytheistic religion
- One who has little or no religion
- One who delights in sensual pleasures and material goods
- An irreligious or hedonistic person
- Traditional designation of a practitioner of classical polytheisms.
- Synonyms: gentile, idolater, idolator, heathen
- Related Words: atheist, giaour, infidel, misbeliever, miscreant, nonbeliever, unbeliever; non-Christian, non-Jew, non-Muslim; neo-pagan, polytheist
- Religion Terms: Zen, antinomian, avatar, gnosticism, illuminati, ineffable, karma, koan, mantra
- Pagan rituals: Christmas (Winter Solstice), Valentine's Day (Lupercus: Hunter of Wolves), Mother/Father's Day (Queen of Heaven/Weeping

for Tammuz), Easter Sunday (Ishtar, Queen of Heaven), Hallowe'en (All Soul's Day), Thanksgiving (Cerilia - Ceres, goddess of harvest), Christmas cookies and milk (leaving presents for Nimrod's widow), Christmas Tree with Christmas Balls (Tammuz erect masculinity/genitals), Easter Egg/rabbit (goddess of fertility), Sunday Services (worship of Sun god), etc.

Be not deceived. Speak honest of praise, obedience and worship in obedience and love to Yahovah and His Word instead of false words spoken in celebration and honor of false gods.

Astrology – Isa 47:13, Jer 10:2, Da 1:20, 2:2,10, 4:7, 5:7-15

The Merriam-Webster Dictionary: astrology:

- The study of how the positions of the stars and movements of the planets have a supposed influence on events and on the lives and behavior of people
- The divination of the supposed influences of the stars and planets on human affairs and terrestrial events by their positions and aspects
- Divination that consists of interpreting the influence of stars and planets on earthly affairs and human destinies
- Other Occult Terms: augury, censor, invocation, lucidity, metempsychosis, mojo, numinous, preternatural, weird, wraith

Be not deceived. Speak honest words and not words guided by fantastical, occultic influences.

CHAPTER 5 – DOOR POINTS

Unless we are in perfect peace with Yahovah, obeying His commandments and not in sin, we have continual door points. A door point is an entryway for a spirit, a non-corporeal entity which enters into our physical bodies and takes up possession of an area.

Since a non-corporeal spirit is a fallen and cursed angel who no longer has a solid body, they can take up a space as small as a cell or a DNA code.

These spirits from Lucifer's followers have one objective. They enter us to convince us to curse ourselves by leading us astray from Yahovah's commandments. You need to understand. They carry out their assignment from the inside, salvation does not make us immune.

They whisper in our ears, convince our hearts, influence our passions, change our minds and rewrite our DNA with generational sins.

These open doors can be a serious incident, such as a car accident, or being cut off in traffic. A surgical procedure is a door for fear, pain etc. But be aware that it need not be a major incident. Maybe a thunderstorm bothers you, cutting your finger or losing your keys. It can be a horrific scene of death or a loud sudden sound. You worry when your kids are out late or travelling. The list of everyday occurrences can be endless.

Traumas and open doors begin in the womb and end with our death. No one is immune as long as we live in this realm on this earth.

These things that happen to us can be natural events, orchestrated by man and even orchestrated by spirits. Regardless what opens the door, they are not only entranceways for spirits to gain access to our innermost being physically, but if the door remains open, they continue to allow spirits in.

This is neither a strange, nor unbiblical concept. Adam and Eve allowed Lucifer and his fellow fallen angels into this realm, the natural universe, from their second heavens prison.

Yahshua delivered His own people from the bondage of spirits, linking these spirits to specific diseases and mental conditions.

It is the lies of Balaam that are preached from our pulpits teaching the falsehood and misconceptions that once we have been *saved by Jesus we are clean and clean forever.*

This is not what Paul teaches in Romans 7 and 8 where he tells us that we have the man of sin within us. The man of sin is the spirit that convinces us to miss the mark by breaking the commandments of Yahovah.

These door points of incidents must be identified and closed to prevent further access by spirits.

Some of the more common door points are:

Conception: Born out of wedlock, Unwanted, Genetic Problems

In Womb: Rejection from the Mother, Illness in the Mother

Trauma of Birth Process: Breech, Cord around the neck, Circumcision

Separations: Hospitalization (yours, parents or loved ones), Given up for Adoption, Mother/Father away at war, Mother/Father away because of job, Mother/Father abandons child, Death, Moving to a new area, Divorce, loss of grandparents, etc.

Accidents: Near drowning, Choking, car accident, plane accident, falling, door closing on finger, cutting oneself, etc. They also include witnessing these happening to others.

Injuries: Breaking a limb or bone, sprains, cuts, being shot, being stabbed, torture, rape, operations, burns, shrapnel, etc.

Confrontation with: an authority in the Church, the Legal System, rejection by a Girlfriend/Boyfriend, BFF or Relative, Incest, Rape, Molestation, Robbery, SRA, Programming, Divorce of Parents, own Divorce, Barrenness, being the dysfunctional in the family, Fear of Poverty, Financial Loss, Poverty, loss of Spouse, loss of Friends, loss of Parent, loss of Child, parents speaking Fear, lies from Parents, lies from Siblings, Verbal Abuse, Emotional Abuse, Physical Abuse, Sexual Abuse, coarse Jesting, Victimization, being the family Scapegoat, witnessing violence, living in a Foster Home or Orphanage, Military Service, being in a Boarding School, being in a

Juvenile Home, being in Prison, keeping Family Secrets, being Afraid, being Anxious, Unfulfilled Expectations, Broken Dreams (Prov 13:12), etc.

Physical Ills: Sickness, Disease, being Crippled, Tattoo, Burning, Cutting, Masochism, Deformity, Markings, Pain, etc.

Other Door Point Entryways: Early Illnesses, Dental Trauma, Rejection due to Physical Differences, Rejection due to Emotional Differences, rejection by Authority Figures such as Teachers, Bosses, Pastors, Doctors, Government, Legal System, Friends, Children, Strangers, etc.

Spiritual Entryways: Soul Ties, False Teachings, False Ceremonies, Dedications to other than Yahovah, Oaths, Dedications to other than Yahovah, Curses, Self-Curses, etc. (see book by author on SOUL TIES)

CHAPTER 6 – SPECIFIC SCRIPTURES

Curses: Proverbs 26:2 – Everything happens for a reason. Something from our generations or own life. Deuteronomy 28 lists diseases and curses that come upon people for breaking Yahovah's Torah. Also, curses will come from words spoken against us. It could go back many generations. The curses is now genetic. Words are spirit, whether blessing or curses.

Fear: 2 Timothy 1:7 – Yahovah has not given us a spirit of Fear. It comes from the enemy, HaSatan

Critical and Perverse Lips: Proverbs 4:24 – Being critical and/or perverse cause problems in our bones

Death: Proverbs 12:1 – He that hates reproof shall die. We have been given the tools to be free and disease free by repentance through Yahovah

Shame to a Husband: Proverbs 12:4 – A woman who shames her husband brings problems to his bones

Hopelessness: Proverbs 13:12 – Depression, Self-Pity, Doubt, Unbelief

Envy: Proverbs 14:30 – Envy will rot our bones

Broken Spirit: Proverbs 17:22 – Dries up the bones as in Brittle Bones, Allergies and Fear

Death and Life: Proverbs 18:21 – Death and Life are in the power of the tongue – repent of our sins and/or generational sins and we shall see health

Chapter 7 – Curses

Below is a very limited list of curses. Curses can be any promise an ancestor made to a god of their choosing, perhaps to promise or dedicate their progeny to the curse of servitude to a false god.

In ancient times fathers, tribes, villages, etc. promised their child and family line to whoever would fill their bellies or promise them good fortune.

These curses, promises, dedications, etc., embed themselves into our DNA and influence our lives.

We can break these curses off ourselves as well our children under the age of accountability. If our children are over the age of accountability, they must break them off themselves.

Curses also come by our own words, continual thoughts or embraced beliefs as well as breaking Yahovah's Commands or Torah.

By our own deeds and actions as well as the deeds and actions of our ancestors, we bring curse upon ourselves. Below is a sampling of actions, beliefs and deeds that bring about a curse.

- Abortion or Causing Unborn To Die
- Adding To or Taking Away From Bible
- Adultery

- African gods
- All gods other than Yahovah
- All gods who try to take the place of Yahovah
- American Indian Curses
- Asian gods
- Australian gods
- Bastard
- Being Carnally Minded
- Bestiality
- Biblical Curses Not listed Above
- Blaspheming LORD'S NAME - Yahovah
- Bless You Spirits
- Broken Vows
- Cabalistic Magic
- Catholic or Rote Prayers – really just learned chants
- Charismatic Witchcraft
- Cheating People Out of Property
- Children Rebelling
- Chinese gods
- Choosing That Which GOD Delights Not In
- Crescent Moon and Star
- Cursed Objects
- Cursing
- Cursing Parents
- Cursing Rulers
- Deceiving
- Defiling The Sabbath
- Destruction of Family Priesthood
- Dishonoring Parents
- Disobedience to Bible
- Disobedience to the Torah – Law of Yahovah

- Doing The Work of GOD Deceitfully
- Eastern Star
- Egyptian Ankh
- Egyptian gods
- Eight Pointed Star
- Emerods
- European gods
- Eurpoean gods
- Failing To Give Glory to Yahovah
- Failure and Poverty
- False Prophets
- False Swearing
- Family Disorder
- Following Horoscopes
- Fortune Telling
- Freemasonry
- Friendship Hex
- Fugitive and Vagabond
- Gods other than Yahovah
- Graven Images
- Harlotry, Prostitution
- Hatred
- Having Children out of Wedlock – The Bastard Curse
- Hearkening to Wives Rather Than GOD
- Hexagram
- Homosexuals and Lesbians
- Horoscopes
- House of Wickedness
- Idol Worship
- Idolatry
- Improper Family Structure

- Incest
- Incest With Sister or Mother
- Intercourse During Menstruation
- Irish Shamrock Hex
- Italian Horn
- Keeping Cursed Objects
- Kidnapping
- Leprechaun's Staff
- Lesbians
- Looking To World For Help – including medical assistance
- Losing Virginity Before Marriage
- Loving Cursing
- Making Graven Images
- Masonic Symbols
- Mexican gods
- Mistreating GOD's Chosen People
- Mogen David
- Murder
- Murder Secretly or For Hire
- Murdering Indirectly
- Necromancers
- Non-productivity
- North American gods
- Norwegian gods
- Not Disciplining Children
- Not Giving To Poor
- Not Preventing Death
- Occult Curses
- Offending Children
- Oppressing Strangers, Widows, Orphans
- Oral and Anal Sex

- Pentacle
- Pentagram
- Perversion of the Gospel
- Pride
- Prince of Occult
- Prince of Southern Curses
- Putting Trust In Man
- Rape
- Rebelling Against Leaders
- Refusing To Do Torah - THE WORD OF GOD
- Refusing To Fight For GOD
- Refusing To Warn Sinners
- Religious gods – Christian, Catholic, Islamic, etc.
- Rewarding Evil For Good
- Robbing GOD of Tithes
- Sacrificing Humans
- Sacrificing to Gods
- Seances
- Sin Worthy of Death
- Sodomy
- South American gods
- Spiritual Blindness
- Spiritual Witchcraft
- Stealing
- Striking Parents
- Stubbornness and Rebellion
- Swearing Falsely By Yahovah
- Taking Advantage of Blind
- Teaching Rebellion Against Yahovah
- The Distelfink
- Touching the Anointed of Yahovah
- Turning Someone Away From Torah

- Turning Someone Away From Yahovah
- Twelve Petal Rosette
- Unicorn's Horn
- Voodoo Curses
- White Magic
- Wicked Balances
- Willing Deceivers
- Witchcraft
- Your Lucky Stars
- Zodiac

There are too many issues and gods to list. You know your culture better than an outsider. Any and every belief and god that does not line up with Torah is a god and belief that needs to be repented of.

It is that simple.

Frequently Occurring Generational Sins, Curses, and Patterns:

- Abandonment
- Abuse: emotional, physical, mental, sexual
- Addictions
- Anger, rage, violence
- Control, possessiveness, manipulation
- Emotional dependency
- Fears of all kinds
- Idolatry
- Money extremes such as greed and lack
- Not caring for children
- Parents and children exchange roles
- Physical infirmities
- Pride, Rebellion
- Rejection, Insecurity

- Religious bondage, Cults
- Sexual sin and perversion
- Unbelief
- Unworthiness, Low self-esteem, Inferiority
- Satanism, Witchcraft, Occult

Generational curses can cause us to be drawn to particular types of sins. The enemy knows these curses, our weaknesses, and he pushes us to curse ourself from obedience to the Word of Yahovah. HaSatan willingly takes advantage of all openings we give him to keep us in sin.

Curses come into our lives from three sources:

- Disobedience to the Word of Yahovah, Torah
- Words spoken against us by others
    - Current or generational
- Words spoken against ourselves

CURSES IN FAMILY LINES:

> **Exodus 34: 6-7** ADONAI passed before him and proclaimed: "YUD-HEH-VAV-HEH!!! Yud-Heh-Vav-Heh [ADONAI] is God, merciful and compassionate, slow to anger, rich in grace and truth; showing grace to the thousandth generation, forgiving offenses, crimes and sins; yet not exonerating the guilty, but causing the negative effects of the parents' offenses to be experienced by their children and grandchildren, and even by the third and fourth generations."

Exodus clearly shows that the sins of the fathers are passed down to the fourth generation of a family line. The loophole is that if the effects of the curse and the sin in the family line is not repented of, then each generation renews the time frame. It is a never ending loop. This is the way it travels through a family line for thousands of years.

It may hide for a generation, but it will come out in the next. These sins have to be repented of and the spirits cast out to break the generational curse of the sin.

SECTION 2
DISEASES AND THEIR
SPIRITUAL ROOTS

CHAPTER 8 – A

Accident Prone: *Spirits:* Low Self-Image, Fear from Molestation and Abuse. You must forgive Abuser and Molester.

Acne – Adolescent: *Spirits:* Fear of Rejection by Peers. You must forgive Parents, Family and Peers.

Acne – Systolic: *Spirits:* Unresolved Bitterness, Conflict between Victim and a close Female figure. You must forgive the female figure in question.

Acoustic Neuroma: *Spirits:* Stress, Anxiety and Fear. You must repent of the specific Fear(s), Stress and Anxiety. Be specific.

Acute Low Back Problems – Adults: *Spirits:* Worry, Double-Mindedness, Anger, Fear, Stress, Anxiety, Critical Spirit, and Insecurity.

ADD – Attention Deficit Disorder: *Spirits:* Self-Hatred, Self-Bitterness, Deaf and Dumb Spirit, Confusion, Rebellion, Occultism, Self-Rejection, Guilt and Gender Disorientation causing Double-Mindedness. You must repent of all these issues generationally as well.

Addictive Eating: *Spirits:* Fear, Stress and Anxiety.

Addison's Disease: *Spirits:* Worry, Double-Mindedness, Anger, Fear, Stress, Anxiety, Critical Spirit, Insecurity, Self-Hatred, Self-Guilt, Self-Conflict, Self-Rejection, Self-Bitterness and Self-Conflict. The person attacks themselves spiritually so the body attacks itself physically by sending white corpuscles to attack our body parts. Auto-immune disease

ADHD – Attention Deficit Hyperactivity Disorder: *Spirits:* Fear, Stress and Anxiety. Worry, Double-Mindedness, Anger, Critical Spirit, and Insecurity.

Adolescent Acne: *Spirits:* Fear of Rejection by Peers. You must forgive Parents, Family and Peers.

Adult On-Set Diabetes: *Spirits:* Self-Rejection, Self-Bitterness and Self-Hatred from long term Rejection, Abuse, Abandonment from a Parent, Guardian or Spouse, Guilt, Self-Bitterness, believing you are not worthy to be accepted. You must forgive your parents for abandoning you and not giving you the time, love and attention you needed.

Adultery: *Sin:* Causes stomach problems and leg problems.

Aggressiveness: *Spirits:* Lack of Proper Nurturing in Childhood, Self-Hatred, Self-Rejection and Guilt. This is also a High Serotonin problem from Fear, Stress, Anxiety and Conflict

Agoraphobia: *Spirits:* Fear, Anxiety and Stress

Alcoholism: *Spirits:* Generational Addictive Personality. Generational Spirit of Addiction. You must look into all sides of your family to find the root cause of this problem.

Allergies: *Spirits:* Broken Spirit, No Fear of the Lord, Separation from Yahovah, Unforgiveness and Open door of trauma. Allergies are connected to dried-up bone marrow which is caused by Long-term Fear, Stress and Anxiety. (Deut. 28:65-68)

ALS – Amyotrophic Lateral Sclerosis: *Spirits:* Rejection, Self-Rejection, Self-Hatred, Heaviness, Oppression, Spirit and Curse of Death, Hell and Destruction

Always Cold: *Spirits:* Spirit of Palsy, Spirit of Candor

Alzheimer Disease: *Spirits:* Self-Hatred, Guilt and all Self Spirits (Self-Anger, Self-Bitterness, etc.)

Amenorrhea: *Spirits:* Fear, Stress and Anxiety

Amyotrophic Lateral Sclerosis – ALS: *Spirits:* Rejection, Self-Rejection, Self-Hatred, Heaviness, Oppression, Spirit and Curse of Death, Hell and Destruction.

Anaphylaxis – Panic Attacks: *Spirits:* Fear, Stress and Anxiety

Aneurysm: *Spirits:* Unresolved Anger, Rage, Resentment, Hostility, Bitterness, Unresolved Rage, Fear, Stress, Anxiety and Spirit of Stroke.

Angina: *Spirits:* Unresolved Anger, Rage, Resentment, Hostility with great Bitterness, Fear, Stress and Anxiety.

Angina Pectoris: *Spirits:* Fear, Stress and Anxiety.

Ankylosing Spondylitis: *Spirits:* Self-Hatred, Self-Guilt, Self-Conflict, Self-Rejection, Self-Bitterness and Fear, Stress and Anxiety. The person attacks themselves spiritually so the body attacks itself physically by sending white corpuscles to attack our body parts. Auto-immune disease.

Anorexia Nervosa: *Spirits:* Self-Hatred, Self-Rejection, Self-Bitterness, Lack of Self-Esteem, Insecurity, Self-Mutilation, No Value, Bitterness, Self-Death, Unloved, Rejection, Hidden Addiction to Food, Drivenness, Performance, Spirit of Control and Matriarchal Witchcraft

Antigen: *Spirits:* Fear, Stress, Anxiety and Self-Rejection

Antiphospholipid Syndrome: *Spirits:* Self-Hatred, Self-Guilt, Self-Conflict, Self-Rejection, Self-Bitterness, Fear, Stress and Anxiety. The person attacks themselves spiritually so the body attacks itself physically by sending white corpuscles to attack our body parts. Auto-immune disease.

Anti-Unconogen: *Spirits:* Broken Relationships with Yahovah, Self and Others.

Anxiety Attack: *Spirits:* Worry, Double-Mindedness, Anger, Fear, Stress, Anxiety, Critical Spirit, and Insecurity.

Anxiety Disorder: *Spirits:* Worry, Double-Mindedness, Anger, Fear, Stress, Anxiety, Critical Spirit, and Insecurity. **Anxiety:** The main root of Anxiety is Fear.

AOBS – Atypical Organic Brain Syndrome: *Spirits:* Fear, Stress and Anxiety

Areata: *Spirits:* Self-Hatred, Self-Guilt, Self-Conflict, Self-Rejection, Self-Bitterness, Fear, Stress and Anxiety. The person attacks themselves spiritually so the body attacks itself physically by sending white corpuscles to attack our body parts. Auto-immune disease

Arrhythmia – Heart: *Spirits:* Worry, Double-Mindedness, Anger, Fear, Stress, Anxiety, Critical Spirit, and Insecurity.

Arteries, Hardening: *Spirits:* Self-Rejection, Self-Bitterness, and Self-Hatred.

Arthritis: *Spirits:* Bitterness against others, Worry, Double-Mindedness, Anger, Fear, Stress, Anxiety, Critical Spirit, and Insecurity.

Arthritis – Osteo: *Spirits:* Self-Bitterness, Guilt

Arthritis – Psoriatic: *Spirits:* Worry, Double-Mindedness, Anger, Fear, Stress, Anxiety, Critical Spirit, and Insecurity.

Arthritis – Rheumatoid: *Spirits:* Bitterness and Unforgiveness toward another (dead or alive), Self-Hatred, Self-Guilt, Self-Conflict, Self-Rejection, Self-Bitterness, Fear, Stress and Anxiety. The person attacks themselves spiritually so the body attacks itself physically by sending white corpuscles to attack our body parts. Auto-immune disease

Arthritis – Simple: *Spirits:* Bitterness against others

Asthma: *Spirits:* Fear, Stress, Anxiety, Self-Hatred, Bitterness, Self-Rejection, Lack of Self-Esteem, Anxiety, Self-Hatred, Guilt, Stress, Avoidance, Fear of Abandonment, Bitterroot Judgments, Unforgiveness (towards parents/spouse, ex-spouse, employers, abusers, molesters, etc.), Insecurity.

Attention Deficit Disorder – ADD: *Spirits:* Self-Hatred, Self-Bitterness, Deaf and Dumb Spirit, Confusion, Rebellion, Occultism, Self-Rejection, Guilt and Gender Disorientation causing Double-Mindedness.

Attention Deficit Hyperactivity Disorder – ADHD: *Spirits:* Fear, Stress and Anxiety.

Atypical Organic Brain Syndrome – AOBS: *Spirits:* Fear, Stress and Anxiety

Autism: *Spirits:* Rejection and Rebellion.

Autoimmune Disease: *Spirits:* Bitterness and Unforgiveness toward another (dead or alive), Self-Rejection, Guilt, Self-Hatred, Self-Conflict, Self-Rejection, Self-Bitterness, Anxiety, Stress, Fear, Stress and Anxiety. The person attacks themselves spiritually so the body attacks itself physically by sending white corpuscles to attack our body parts.

CHAPTER 9 – B

Back Pain – Degenerative Disc: *Spirits:* Self-Bitterness, Addictive Personality, Unresolved Issues, Conflict with another Female (Mother, Sister, Aunt), Self-Rejection, Self-Conflict, Spirit of Kundalini and Divination when injury is not present.

Back Problems: *Spirits:* Fear, Stress, Anxiety, Fear of Future, and Self-Rejection. Occult, Divination, Kundalini

Back Problems – Lower: *Spirits:* Fear, Stress, Anxiety, Fear of Future, and Self-Rejection. Divination (Kundalini, the snake is wrapped around the lower back/stomach area)

Back Problems – Upper: *Spirits:* Fear, Stress, Anxiety, Fear of Future, Self-Rejection, and Occult

Bareness: *Spirits:* Fear, Stress, Anxiety, Abandonment, Rejection, Self-Rejection, Self-Bitterness, and Self-Hatred, Inherited Curse, Adultery. Jealous husband brings Curse on the wife.

Behcet's Disease: *Spirits*: Fear, Stress, Anxiety, Self-Hatred, Self-Guilt, Self-Conflict, Self-Rejection, and Self-Bitterness. The person attacks themselves spiritually so the body attacks itself physically by sending white corpuscles to attack our body parts. Auto-immune

Biblar –Amyotrophic Lateral Sclerosis – ALS: *Spirits:* Rejection, Self-Rejection, Self-Hatred, Heaviness,

Oppression, Spirit of Death, Curse of Death, Hell, Destruction, Guilt, Fear, Stress and Anxiety

Binge Eating Disorder: *Spirits:* Worry, Double-Mindedness, Anger, Fear, Stress, Anxiety, Critical Spirit, and Insecurity.

Bipolar Disorder: *Spirits:* Generational Fear, Stress, Anxiety, Spirit of Infirmity, False Religion, Occult, Witchcraft, SRA (Satanic Ritual Abuse), Ouija Boards, etc., Male Victimization causes Manic Depression in women. An inherited Genetic issue – ask Yahovah to reorder the 27th lower right-hand side of the X-Chromosome genetics to restore the genetic structure.

Bladder Problems: *Spirits:* Fear, Stress and Anxiety

Blindness: *Spirits:* Bitterroot Judgments, Unforgiveness (towards Parents, Spouse, Ex-Spouse, Employers, Abusers, Molesters, etc.)

Bloating Stomach: *Spirits:* Fear, Stress, Anxiety, Abandonment, Rejection, Self-Rejection, Self-Bitterness, and Self-Hatred, Inherited Curse. Jealous husband brings Curse on the wife. Adultery.

Blood Diseases: *Spirits:* Fear, Stress, Anxiety, Spirit of Cancer, Nerve Destroyer, Kidney Destroyer and Generational Familiar Spirits.

Blood Pressure – High: *Spirits:* Fear, Stress and Anxiety

Blood Sugar, High – Diabetes: *Spirits:* Extreme Rejection, Fear of Man, Hatred of Man, Self-Hatred, Self-Rejection,

Self-Bitterness, Guilt and Rejection by a Significant Male Figure

Blood Sugar, Low – Hypoglycemia: *Spirits:* Fear, Stress, Anxiety, Self-Hatred, Self-Rejection and Performance.

Bone Problems: *Spirits:* Iniquity of the Fathers, Iniquity, Sorrow in Relationships with Yahovah, Self or Others, Disobedience to Yahovah's word, Torah, Grief (Ps 31:10), Curse, Soul-Ties (Ps 38:3), Envy (Prov 14:30), Adultery (Prov 12:4)

Bowel Disease: *Spirits:* Fear, Stress, Anxiety, Abandonment, Rejection, Self-Rejection, Self-Bitterness, and Self-Hatred, Adultery, Inherited Curse and Jealous Husband brings Curse on the wife

Brain Fog in CFS: *Spirits:* Fear, Stress, Anxiety, Lack of Self-Esteem and Guilt.

Brain Fog in MCS/EI: *Spirits:* Fear, Stress, Anxiety, Lack of Self-Esteem and Guilt.

Breakdown of Marriage: *Spirits:* Religious Pride, Anger, Not Honoring Parents (Breaking Torah), Divorce (will cause us to live in Poverty for a season whether Spiritually, Mentally or Financially)

Breast Cancer: *Spirits:* 10% of all women have a Genetic Code Defect, Deep Rooted Bitterness and Resentment either with a Mother or Sisters

Breast Cysts: *Spirits:* Conflict with Mother, Self-Rejection, Self-Hatred, Self-Bitterness, Unresolved Bitterness, Conflict with a close Female Figure (Mother, Sister, Mother-in-law), Generational Violation of the laws of Niddah – Sexual Intercourse during menstruation – brings on barrenness, Fornication, Pornography, Abortion, Affairs, Soul-Ties, Flashbacks of Past Relationships, Comparing Spouse with Parents, Oral Sex and Masturbation (Homosexual Act – Witchcraft).

Bulimia: *Spirits:* Self-Hatred, Drivenness, Performance, Control, Matriarchal Witchcraft, Self-Rejection, Self-Bitterness, Lack of Self-Esteem, Insecure, Self-Mutilation, Feel of No Value, Unloved, Fear, Stress, Anxiety and Rejection

Bulimia Nervosa – High Serotonin Problem: *Spirits:* Self-Hatred, Drivenness, Performance, Control, Matriarchal Witchcraft, Self-Rejection, Self-Bitterness, Lack of Self-Esteem, Insecure, Self-Mutilation, Feel of No Value, Unloved. Fear, Stress, Anxiety and Rejection

Bursitis: *Spirits:* Fear, Stress, Anxiety, Guilt and Self-Hatred

CHAPTER 10 – C

Can't Get Warm: *Spirits:* Spirit of Palsy and Spirit of Candor

Cancer: *Spirits:* Fear, Stress, Anxiety, Long-term Bitterness, Hatred, Anger, Retaliation, Helplessness, Broken Relationship with God, self or others, Bitterroot Judgments and Unforgiveness (towards Parents, Spouse, Ex-Spouse, Employers, Abusers, Molesters, etc.)

Cancer – Breast: *Spirits:* Unresolved Bitterness or Conflict between a Woman and Close Female Figure

Cancer – Colon: *Spirits:* Bitterness, Slander with the Tongue and Dumping on others

Cancer – Liver: *Spirits:* Fornication, Adultery and Addiction to Pornography (Prov. 7:21-23)

Cancer – Ovarian: *Spirits:* Self-Bitterness, Promiscuity and Self-Hatred at being Female

Cancer – Pancreas: *Spirits:* Fear, Stress, Anxiety, Spirit of Pancreatic Cancer, Generational Familiar Spirits, Self-Bitterness, Self-Hatred and Self- Rejection. Diagnosed in early stages as Diabetes.

Cancer – Prostate: *Spirits:* Anger, Guilt, Self-Hatred, Self-Bitterness, Self-Conflict with male identity and Self-Rejection

Cancer – Skin: *Spirits:* Inherited Long-term Bitterness, Hatred, Anger, Retaliation, Helplessness, Broken Relationship with Yahovah, Self or Others. Can be caused by not protecting the skin from the sun.

Cancer – Throat: *Spirits:* Broken Spirit, Unforgiveness, Unresolved Conflict with Others and Self, Fear, Stress and Anxiety

Cancer – Uterine: *Spirits:* Need to be loved causing Promiscuity and Uncleanness

Candida Albicans: *Spirits:* Fear, Stress, Anxiety and Broken Relationship

Candidiasis: *Spirits:* Fear, Stress and Anxiety

Cardiomyopathy: *Spirits:* Fear, Stress, Anxiety, Self-Hatred, Self-Guilt, Self-Rejection, Self-Bitterness and Self-Conflict. The person attacks themselves spiritually so the body attacks itself physically by sending white corpuscles to attack our body parts. Auto-immune

Cartilage Degeneration: *Spirits:* Self-Bitterness and Guilt

Catatonia: *Spirits:* Fear, Stress, Anxiety and Broken by a Past Relationship

Catatonic Reality – Panic Attacks: *Spirits:* Fear, Stress and Anxiety

Catecholamine's: *Spirits:* Fear, Stress and Anxiety

Celiac Sprue-Dermatitis: *Spirits:* Self-Hatred, Self-Guilt, Self-Conflict, Self-Rejection, Self-Bitterness, Self-Conflict,

Fear, Stress and Anxiety. The person attacks themselves spiritually so the body attacks itself physically by sending white corpuscles to attack our body parts. Auto-immune

Cell Wall Rigidity Disease: *Spirits:* Fear, Stress, Anxiety, Self-Hatred and Guilt

Cell Wall Rigidity – Malabsorption: *Spirits:* Fear, Stress and Anxiety

Cerebral Palsy: *Not a Spirit:* Ask for a creative miracle from Yahovah.

CFIDS – Dysfunction Syndrome: *Spirits:* Self-Hatred, Self-Guilt, Self-Conflict, Self-Rejection, Self-Bitterness, Fear, Stress and Anxiety. The person attacks themselves spiritually so the body attacks itself physically by sending white corpuscles to attack our body parts. Auto-immune

Chemical Allergies: *Spirits:* Broken Heart, Occultism, Fear, Stress and Anxiety

Cholesterol – High: *Spirits:* Fear, Stress, Anxiety, Paranoia, Self-Bitterness, Self-Hostility and Self-Anger

Cholesterol – Too Low: *Spirits:* Lack of Proper Nurturing in childhood, Self-Hatred, Self-Rejection and Guilt

Chronic Depression: *Spirits:* Suppressed Anger and Distrust

Chronic Diseases: *Spirits:* Bitterroot Judgments and Unforgiveness (towards Parents, Spouse, Ex-Spouse, Employers, Abusers, Molesters, etc.)

Chronic Fatigue Syndrome – CFS: *Spirits:* Fear, Stress, Anxiety, Breakdown in Relationship with a Parent or Guardian resulting in Exhaustion, Drivenness to meet the Expectations of a Parent for Love and Acceptance, Abandonment, Rejection, Hope Deferred, Lost Hope, Broken Spirit, Self-Hatred, Self-Bitterness, Self-Guilt, Failure, Don't Measure Up, Never Having Expectations Fulfilled, Self-Conflict and Self-Rejection. The person attacks themselves spiritually so the body attacks itself physically by sending white corpuscles to attack our body parts. Auto-immune

Chronic Inflammatory Demyelinating Polyneuropathy – CIDP: *Spirits:* Self-Hatred, Self-Guilt, Self-Conflict, Self-Rejection, Self-Bitterness, Fear, Stress and Anxiety. The person attacks themselves spiritually so the body attacks itself physically by sending white corpuscles to attack our body parts. Auto-immune

Chronic Pain: *Spirits:* Lack of Proper Nurturing in Childhood, Self-Hatred, Self-Rejection, Guilt, Worry, Double-Mindedness, Anger, Fear, Stress, Anxiety, Critical Spirit, and Insecurity

Chronic Sinus Infection: *Spirits:* Fear, Stress and Anxiety

Churg-Strauss Syndrome: *Spirits:* Self-Hatred, Self-Guilt, Self-Rejection, Self-Bitterness, Self-Conflict, Fear, Stress and Anxiety. The person attacks themselves spiritually so the body attacks itself physically by sending white corpuscles to attack our body parts. Auto-immune

Cicatricial Pemphigoid: *Spirits:* Self-Hatred, Self-Guilt, Self-Rejection, Self-Bitterness, Self-Conflict, Fear, Stress and Anxiety. The person attacks themselves spiritually so the body attacks itself physically by sending white corpuscles to attack our body parts. Auto-immune

CIDP – Chronic Inflammatory Demyelinating Polyneuropathy: *Spirits:* Self-Hatred, Self-Guilt, Self-Rejection, Self-Bitterness, Self-Conflict, Fear, Stress and Anxiety. The person attacks themselves spiritually so the body attacks itself physically by sending white corpuscles to attack our body parts. Auto-immune

Cirrhosis of the Liver: *Spirits:* Bitterness, Self-Rejection, Lack of Self-Esteem, Anxiety, Self-Hatred, Guilt, Fear, Stress and Anxiety

Claustrophobia: *Spirits:* Fear, Stress and Anxiety

Cluster Headaches: *Spirits:* Fear, Stress and Anxiety

Cocaine Addiction: *Spirits:* Need to be Loved, Guilt and Condemnation.

Cold: *Spirits:* Easily Offended, Broken Heart, Self-Doubt, Guilt, Spirit of Infirmity, Fear, Stress and Anxiety

Cold – Can't Get Warm: *Spirits:* Spirit of Palsy and Spirit of Candor

Cold Agglutinin Disease: *Spirits:* Self-Hatred, Self-Guilt, Self-Rejection, Self-Bitterness, Self-Conflict, Fear, Stress and Anxiety. The person attacks themselves spiritually so the body attacks itself physically by sending white corpuscles to attack our body parts. Auto-immune

Colic: *Spirits:* Inherited Fear, Stress and Anxiety.

Collateral Ligament Injuries: *Spirits:* Worry, Double-Mindedness, Anger, Critical Spirit, Insecurity, Fear, Stress and Anxiety.

Colon Cancer: *Spirits:* Bitterness, Slander with the Tongue, Dumping on Others and Unforgiveness

Color Blindness: *Spirits:* Deaf and Dumb Spirit; Gender Disorientation, Double-Mindedness, Confusion, Rebellion, Occultism, Self-Rejection, Self-Hatred and Guilt

Compromised Immune System: *Spirits:* Broken Heart

Compulsive Behavior: *Spirits:* Self-Hatred, Self-Rejection, all the Self Spirits (Self-Anger, etc.)

Compulsive Liar: *Spirits:* Lying, Mistrust of God, Insecurity, Self-Preservation, Selfishness, Fear, Stress and Anxiety

Confusion: *Spirits:* Fear, Stress, Anxiety, Double-Mindedness, Occult, White Magic, Black Magic, Paganism, Earth Worship, Wicca, New Age, Secret Societies, Freemasonry, Lodges, Fraternities, Sororities, Horoscopes, Astrology, Ouija Boards, Tarot Cards, etc., and Spirit of Diabetes.

Congenital Heart Disease: *Spirits:* Inherited Genetic Curse.

Congestive Heart Failure: *Spirits:* Fear, Stress, Anxiety, Bitterness, Self-Rejection, Lack of Self-Esteem, Self-Hatred and Guilt

Constipation: *Spirits:* Fear, Stress and Anxiety.

Consumption: *Spirits:* Bitterroot Judgments and Unforgiveness (towards Parents, Spouse, Ex-Spouse, Employers, Abusers, Molesters, etc.)

Control: *Spirits:* Fear, Stress and Anxiety.

Controlling: *Spirit Family Notes:* The root of a controlling personality is Fear, Stress, Anxiety and Witchcraft

Coronary Artery Disease: *Spirits:* (Luke 21:26) Fear, Stress, Anxiety, Self-Rejection, Self-Bitterness and Self-Hatred.

Coronary Heart Disorders: *Spirits:* Worry, Double-Mindedness, Anger, Fear, Stress, Anxiety, Critical Spirit, and Insecurity.

CREST Syndrome: *Spirits:* Fear, Stress, Anxiety, Self-Hatred, Self-Guilt, Self-Rejection, Self-Bitterness and Self-Conflict. The person attacks themselves spiritually so the body attacks itself physically by sending white corpuscles to attack our body parts. Auto-immune

Crohn's Disease: *Spirits:* Fear, Stress, Anxiety, Self-Hatred, Self-Guilt, Self-Rejection, Self-Bitterness, Self-Conflict, Guilt of not Performing Perfectly enough to gain Love, Affection and Acceptance of an Unloving Parent, Extreme Self-Rejection, Hopelessness, Conflict from massive Rejection,

Abandonment, Lack of Self-Esteem, Drivenness to meet the Expectation of Another, Co-Dependency and False Burden Bearing. The person attacks themselves spiritually so the body attacks itself physically by sending white corpuscles to attack our body parts. Auto-immune

Cysts – Breast: *Spirits:* Unresolved Bitterness, Conflict between a Woman and a close Female Figure (Mother, Sister, Mother-in-law), Generational Violation of the laws of Niddah – Sexual Intercourse during menses – brings on the curse of barrenness, Fornication, Pornography, Abortion, Affairs, Soul-Ties, Flashbacks of Past Relationships, Comparing Spouse with Parents, Oral Sex and Masturbation (a Homosexual Act – Witchcraft)

Cysts – Ovarian: *Spirits:* Unresolved Bitterness or Conflict between a Woman and a close Female Figure (Mother, Sister, Mother-in-law), Generational Violation of the laws of Niddah – Sexual Intercourse during menses – brings on the curse of barrenness. Fornication, Pornography, Abortion, Affairs, Soul-Ties, Flashbacks of Past Relationships, Comparing Spouse with Parents, Oral Sex and Masturbation (a Homosexual act – Witchcraft)

CHAPTER 11 – D

Death - Premature: *Spirits:* Hate and Self-Hate

Degenerative Disc: *Spirits:* Self-Bitterness, Addictive Personality, Unresolved Issue, Conflict with another Female (Mother, Sister, Aunt), Self-Rejection and Self-Conflict, Spirit of Kundalini and Divination when injury is not present

Degenerative Disc – Back Pain: *Spirits*: Self-Bitterness, Addictive Personality, Unresolved Issues, Conflict with another Female (Mother, Sister, Aunt), Self-Rejection, Self-Conflict, Spirit of Kundalini and Divination when injury is not present

Depression: *Spirits:* Worry, Double-Mindedness, Anger, Critical Spirit, Insecurity, Lack of Proper Nurturing in Childhood, Stress, Anxiety, Double-Mindedness, Occult, White Magic, Black Magic, Paganism, Earth Worship, Wicca, New Age, Secret Societies, Freemasonry, Lodges, Fraternities, Sororities, Horoscopes, Astrology, Ouija Boards, Tarot Cards, etc., and Spirit of Diabetes

Depression – Chronic: *Spirits:* Suppressed Anger and Distrust

Depression – Postpartum: *Spirits:* Lack of Proper Nurturing in Childhood, Self-Hatred, Self-Rejection, Guilt, Worry, Double-Mindedness, Anger, Anxiety, Fear, Stress, Anxiety, Critical Spirit and Insecurity

Depression During Pregnancy: *Spirits:* Lack of Proper Nurturing in childhood, Self-Hatred, Self-Rejection and Guilt

Dermatitis: *Spirits:* Worry, Double-Mindedness, Anger, Fear, Stress, Anxiety, Critical Spirit, and Insecurity.

Dermatitis – Neuro: *Spirits:* Fear, Stress and Anxiety

Dermatomyositis: *Spirits:* Fear, Stress, Anxiety, Self-Hatred, Self-Guilt, Self-Rejection, Self-Bitterness and Self-Conflict. The person attacks themselves spiritually so the body attacks itself physically by sending white corpuscles to attack our body parts. Auto-immune

Despair: *Spirits:* Not knowing one's identity in Yahovah. Root is doubt, Fear, Stress, Anxiety, Unbelief, Spirit of Mistaken Identity. Hopelessness can manifest as Parkinson's Disease.

Diabetes: *Spirits:* Spirit of Infirmity, Fear of Death, Anger, Guilt, Depression, Hopelessness, Doorkeeper of Insulin, Spirits of Torment, Bloodline Curse, Curse of Breaking One's Body, Curse of Slavery, Generational Familiar Spirits, Nerve Destroyer, Kidney Destroyer, Spirits of Itching, Irritation, Incoherent Demon, Worry, Double-Mindedness, Anger, Fear, Stress, Anxiety, Critical Spirit, Insecurity, Extreme Rejection, Self-Hatred, Guilt, Rejection by a significant Male figure, (Father or Husband), Self-Rejection, Self-Hate, Self-Bitterness, Fear of Man, Hatred of Man, Bitterroot Judgments, Unforgiveness (towards Parents, Spouse, Ex-Spouse, Employers, Abusers, Molesters, etc.), and Spirit of Diabetes. This is a ten-armed Spirit seated in the pancreas. The arms must be cut off. They are: Spirit of Migraine/Headache in the head, Spirit of Diabetes in the Kidneys, Eyes, Liver, Bladder, Skin and Lungs, Curse of Asa and Spirit of Candor in the Feet, Deaf and dumb Spirit in the Ears, and Spirit of Impotence in the reproductive areas.

Diabetes – Adult: *Spirits:* Self-Rejection, Self-Bitterness, Self-Hatred, Long term Rejection, Abuse, Abandonment from a Parent, Guardian or Spouse. Guilt, Self-Bitterness, and Believing Not Worthy to be Accepted. Forgive your parents for abandoning you and not giving you the time, love and attention you needed.

Diabetes – High Blood Sugar: *Spirits:* Extreme Rejection, Fear of Man, Hatred of Man, Self-Hatred, Self-Rejection, Self-Bitterness, Guilt and Rejection by a significant Male figure.

Diabetes – Insulin Dependent: *Spirits:* Self-Hatred, Self-Guilt, Self-Conflict, Self-Rejection, Self-Bitterness, Fear, Stress and Anxiety. The person attacks themselves spiritually so the body attacks itself physically by sending white corpuscles to attack our body parts. Auto-immune

Diarrhea: *Spirits:* Fear, Stress and Anxiety

Diminished Smell: *Spirits:* Long term Fear, Stress and Anxiety

Diminished Taste: *Spirits:* Long term Fear, Stress and Anxiety

Disc – Slipped: *Spirits:* Self-Bitterness, Unresolved Issues, Conflict with a Female (Mother), Self-Rejection and Self-

Conflict, Spirit of Kundalini and Divination when injury is not present

Discoid Lupus: *Spirits:* Fear, Stress, Anxiety, Self-Hatred, Self-Guilt, Self-Rejection, Self-Bitterness and Self-Conflict. The person attacks themselves spiritually so the body attacks itself physically by sending white corpuscles to attack our body parts. Auto-immune

Disease: *Spirits:* 50% of all spiritually rooted diseases are Rage and Anger from the Kingdom of Bitterness. Most of the rest are from Fear and Self Spirits (Self-Hate, etc.)

Diuresis: *Spirits:* Fear, Stress, Anxiety and Spirit of Diabetes

Diverticulitis: *Spirits:* Rage, Anger, Fear, Stress and Anxiety.

Dizziness: *Spirits:* Fear, Stress, Anxiety, Self-Hatred and Guilt.

Drivenness: *Spirits:* Stress, Anxiety and Fear, Matriarchal Witchcraft, Occult, Spirit of Control, Unloving Spirit, Wanting to please a Parent in a home of Rejection, Strife, Anger, Not Being Accepted, Not Being Loved and Unrest

Dry Mouth: *Spirits:* Fear, Stress and Anxiety

Dysfunction Syndrome – CFIDS: *Spirits:* Fear, Stress, Anxiety, Self-Hatred, Self-Guilt, Self-Rejection, Self-Bitterness and Self-Conflict. The person attacks themselves spiritually so the body attacks itself physically by sending white corpuscles to attack our body parts. Auto-immune

Dyslexia: *Spirits:* Deaf and Dumb Spirit, Gender Disorientation, Double-Mindedness, Confusion, Rebellion, Occultism, Self-Rejection, Self-Hatred and Guilt

CHAPTER 12 – E

Ear Problems: *Spirits:* Inhibited Hearing, Spirit of Diabetes and Spirit of Deafness.

Ears – Ringing: *Spirits:* Drug overdose, damage from an accident or loud noise opens the door to a spirit of Witchcraft and Occult

Eating – Addictive: *Spirits:* Fear, Stress and Anxiety.

Eating Disorders: *Spirits:* Fear, Stress and Anxiety

Excessive Foot Odor: *Spirits:* Spirit of Palsy and Spirit of Candor

Eczema: *Spirits:* Fear, Stress, Anxiety, (Deut. 28) Curse from disobedience to YAHOVAH's Torah, Self-Hatred, Rejection, Lack of Self-Esteem and Conflict with one's Identity

Edema: *Spirits:* Fear, Stress and Anxiety

EFS – Electromagnetic Field Sensitivity: *Spirits:* Occultism, Stress, Fear and Anxiety. Same as MCS/EI

EI – Environment Illness: *Spirits:* Fear, Stress, Anxiety, Breakdown in Relationship with a Parent or Guardian

Electro Magnetic Field Syndrome – EMF: *Spirits:* Occultism, Stress, Fear and Anxiety. Same as MCS/EI

Electromagnetic Field Sensitivity – EFS: *Spirits:* Occultism, Stress, Fear and Anxiety. Same as MCS/EI

Elevated Cholesterol: *Spirits:* Fear, Stress, Anxiety and Paranoia

EMF – Electro Magnetic Field Syndrome: *Spirits:* Occultism, Stress, Fear and Anxiety. Same as MCS/EI

Emotional Breakdowns: *Spirits:* Fear, Stress, Anxiety, Double-Mindedness, Occult, White Magic, Black Magic, Paganism, Earth Worship, Wicca, New Age, Secret Societies, Freemasonry, Lodges, Fraternities, Sororities, Horoscopes, Astrology, Ouija Boards, Tarot Cards, etc., and Spirit of Diabetes

Emphysema: *Spirits:* Addictive Spirit

Endometriosis: *Spirits:* Self-Rejection and Self-Hatred

Environment Illness – EI: *Spirits:* Fear, Stress, Anxiety, Broken Heart, Occult, and Breakdown in Relationship with a Parent or Guardian.

Environmental Illness – MCS/EI: *Spirits:* Breakup in Relationship with a close Family Member, Physical Abuse, Verbal Abuse, Sexual Abuse, Drivenness to meet expectations of domineering cold Parent to receive their Love, Fear, Stress and Anxiety

Epilepsy: *Spirits:* Deaf and Dumb Spirit and Spirit of Epilepsy

Erection Problems: *Spirits:* Fear, Stress and Anxiety.

Essential Mixed Cryoglobulinemia: *Spirits:* Self-Hatred, Self-Guilt, Self-Conflict, Self-Rejection, Self-Bitterness, Fear, Stress and Anxiety. The person attacks themselves spiritually so the body attacks itself physically by sending white corpuscles to attack our body parts. Auto-immune

Exhaustion: *Spirits:* Fear, Stress and Anxiety

Exploding Blood Vessels: *Spirits:* Unresolved Anger, Rage, Resentment, Hostility, Bitterness, Fear, Stress, Anxiety and Spirit of Stroke

Eye Problems: *Spirits:* Unforgiveness, Grief, Broken Relationships, Occult, Spirit of Burning Ague and Opthamalia. (Ps 6:7, 31:9)

CHAPTER 13 – F

Family Alienation: *Spirits:* Religious Pride, Anger, Not Honoring Parents, and breaking Torah's commands. Divorce will cause us to live in poverty for a season whether spiritually, mentally or financially.

Fatigue: *Spirits:* Fear, Stress and Anxiety, Spirits: Worry, Double-Mindedness, Anger, Fear, Stress, Anxiety, Critical Spirit, and Insecurity. (Isa 40:31, Neh 8:12)

Festering Sores: *Spirits:* Bitterroot Judgments and Unforgiveness (towards Parents, Spouse, Ex-Spouse, Employers, Abusers, Molesters, etc.)

Fever – Severe Burning: *Spirits:* Bitterroot Judgments and Unforgiveness (towards Parents, Spouse, Ex-Spouse, Employers, Abusers, Molesters, etc.)

Fibroid Cysts: *Spirits:* Self-Hatred from Bitterness of a Mother

Fibroid Tumor – Benign: *Spirits:* Self-Bitterness

Fibromyalgia: *Spirits:* Fear, Stress, Anxiety, Broken Relationship with Parent or Guardian, Tension, Depression, Striving, Self-Hatred, Emotional Conflict, Rejection, Lack of Nurturing. Worry, Double-Mindedness, Anger, Critical Spirit, and Insecurity

Fibromyositis: *Spirits:* Self-Hatred, Self-Guilt, Self-Conflict, Self-Rejection, Self-Bitterness, Fear, Stress and Anxiety. The person attacks themselves spiritually so the body attacks itself physically by sending white corpuscles to attack our body parts. Auto-immune

Fibromyalgia-Fibromyositis: *Spirits:* Self-Hatred, Self-Guilt, Self-Rejection, Self-Bitterness, Self-Conflict, Fear, Stress and Anxiety. The person attacks themselves spiritually so the body attacks itself physically by sending white corpuscles to attack our body parts. Auto-immune

Financial Insufficiency: *Spirits:* Continuing Adulterous Affairs, Pornography, Greed, Sexual Immorality, Spirit of Lust, Anger and Rage

Flu: *Spirits:* Fear, Stress, Anxiety, Spirit of Infirmity, Broken heart, Self-Doubt and Guilt

Fluid Retention Diseases: *Spirits:* Fear, Anxiety, Stress, Self-Hatred and Guilt

Foot Swelling: *Spirits:* Spirit of Palsy and Spirit of Candor

Frailty: *Spirits:* Grief, Complaining, Self-Pity, What-About-Me, Disgust, and Dissatisfaction

Frigidity: *Spirits:* Spirit of Diabetes, Fear, Stress, Anxiety, Generational Violation of the laws of Niddah – Sexual Intercourse during a Period, Fornication, Pornography, Abortion, Affairs, Soul-Ties, Flashbacks of Past Relationships, Comparing Spouse with Parents, Oral Sex and Masturbation (a Homosexual Act – Witchcraft) and Uncleanness of sexual identity

Fuzzy Thinking – Panic Attacks: *Spirits:* Fear, Anxiety and Stress

Jessica Jones

Fuzzy Thinking: <u>*Spirits:*</u> Fear, Anxiety and Stress

CHAPTER 14 – G

GAD – Generalized Anxiety Disorder: *Spirits:* Fear, Stress and Anxiety.

Gall Bladder Stone: *Spirits:* Self-Hatred and Self-Rejection and Self-Rejection over being fat

Gastro-Intestinal Problems: *Spirits:* Fear, Anxiety and Stress

Gender Disorientation: *Spirits:* Inversion of Godly order in the home

General Adaptation Syndrome: *Spirits:* Fear, Anxiety and Stress

Generalized Anxiety Disorder – GAD: *Spirits:* Fear, Stress and Anxiety

Genitourinary System: *Spirits:* Diuresis, Impotence, Frigidity and Spirit of Diabetes

Giant Cell Arteritis: *Spirits:* Self-Hatred, Self-Guilt, Self-Rejection, Self-Bitterness, Self-Conflict, Fear, Stress and Anxiety. The person attacks themselves spiritually so the body attacks itself physically by sending white corpuscles to attack our body parts. Auto-imune

Glaucoma: *Spirits:* Fear, Stress, Anxiety, Bitterness, Self-Rejection, Lack of Self-Esteem, Self-Hatred and Guilt

Goiters: *Spirits:* Fear, Stress, Anxiety, Self-Hatred, Self-Rejection and Guilt

Gout: *Spirits:* Extreme Fear, Stress and Anxiety

Graves' Disease: *Spirits:* Very serious Emotional Conflict, Guilt, Fear, Stress, Anxiety, Self-Hatred, Self-Guilt, Self-Rejection, Self-Bitterness and Self-Conflict. The person attacks themselves spiritually so the body attacks itself physically by sending white corpuscles to attack our body parts. Auto-immune

Guillain-Barré: *Spirits:* Stress, Anxiety, Self-Hatred, Self-Guilt, Self-Rejection, Self-Bitterness, Self-Conflict and Fear. The person attacks themselves spiritually so the body attacks itself physically by sending white corpuscles to attack our body parts. Auto-immune

Gulf War Syndrome: *Spirits:* Fear, Stress and Anxiety

CHAPTER 15 – H

Hardening of the Arteries: *Spirits:* Self-Rejection, Self-Bitterness, and Self-Hatred

Hashimoto's Disease: *Spirits:* Self-Hatred, Self-Rejection, Guilt, Fear, Stress and Anxiety

Hashimoto's Thyroiditis: *Spirits:* Self-Hatred, Self-Guilt, Self-Rejection, Self-Bitterness, Self-Conflict, Fear, Stress and Anxiety. The person attacks themselves spiritually so the body attacks itself physically by sending white corpuscles to attack our body parts. Auto-immune

Hatred: *Spirit Family Notes:* Unloving Spirit and Spirit of Death. Part of the Bitterness Kingdom

Hay Fever: *Spirits:* Deep Rooted Fear, Stress, Anxiety and Broken Heart

Headache – Migraine: *Spirits:* Inner Conflict, Guilt, Fear, Stress, Anxiety Self-Conflict, Self-Rejection, Self-Bitterness, Self-Hatred, Internalized Conflict, Spirit of Diabetes, Worry, Double-Mindedness, Anger, Critical Spirit, and Insecurity.

Headache – Tension: *Spirits:* Lack of Proper Nurturing in Childhood, Fear, Stress, Anxiety, Self-Hatred, Self-Rejection, Guilt and Spirit of Diabetes

Heart – Arrhythmia: *Spirits:* Worry, Double-Mindedness, Anger, Chronic Fear, Stress, Anxiety, Critical Spirit and Insecurity

Heart – Coronary Artery Disease: *Spirits:* Luke 21:26 Fear, Stress and Anxiety

Heart – Exploding Blood Vessels: *Spirits:* Unresolved Anger, Rage, Resentment, Hostility, great Bitterness, Fear, Stress, Anxiety and Spirit of Stroke.

Heart – Rhythm Fluttering: *Spirits:* Fear, Stress and Anxiety

Heart Attack: *Spirits:* Fear, Stress, Anxiety, Anger, Rage, Resentment, Unresolved Rage, Anger and Spirit of Stroke

Heart Disease: *Spirits:* Bitterroot Judgments, Unforgiveness (towards Parents, Spouse, Ex-Spouse, Employers, Abusers, Molesters, etc.), Spirit of Dropsy, Fear, Stress, Anxiety, Worry, Double-Mindedness, Anger, Critical Spirit and Insecurity.

Heart Disease – Congenital: *Curse:* Inherited Genetic Curse

Heart Murmur: *Spirits:* This is a Genetic Disease. Generational Fear, Stress and Anxiety. Remove the spiritual root and ask Yahovah to change the genetic code.

Heart Muscle Inflammation: *Spirits:* Fear, Stress, Anxiety and Self-Hatred

Heart Palpitations: *Spirits:* Fear, Stress and Anxiety

Heart Problems: *Spirits:* Unresolved Anger, Rage, Resentment, Hostility, great Bitterness, Fear, Stress and Anxiety.

Heartburn: *Spirits:* Fear, Stress and Anxiety

Heartburn – Mitro Valve Prolapse: *Spirits:* Fear, Stress and Anxiety

Heartburn – Reflux: *Spirits:* Fear, Stress and Anxiety

Hemolytic Anemia: *Spirits:* Self-Hatred, Self-Guilt, Self-Rejection, Self-Bitterness, Self-Conflict, Fear, Stress and Anxiety. The person attacks themselves spiritually so the body attacks itself physically by sending white corpuscles to attack our body parts. Auto-immune

Hemorrhoids: *Spirits:* Fear, Stress, Anxiety, Anger, Rage, Unresolved Anger, Rage, Resentment, Hostility, Bitterness and Spirit of Stroke

Hepatitis: *Spirits:* Self-Hatred, Self-Guilt, Self-Conflict, Self-Rejection, Self-Bitterness, Fear, Stress and Anxiety. The person attacks themselves spiritually so the body attacks itself physically by sending white corpuscles to attack our body parts. Auto-immune

Hereditary Diseases: *Spirits:* Bitterroot Judgments, Unforgiveness (towards Parents, Spouse, Ex-Spouse, Employers, Abusers, Molesters, etc.)

Herpes: *Spirits:* Spirit of Infirmity, Fear, Stress and Anxiety

Hiatal Hernia: *Spirits:* Fear, Stress and Anxiety

High Blood Pressure: *Spirits:* Fear, Stress, Anxiety, Generational Familiar Spirits, Unresolved Rage and Anger

High Blood Sugar – Diabetes: <u>*Spirits:*</u> Extreme Rejection, Fear of Man, Hatred of Man, Self-Hatred, Self-Rejection, Self-Bitterness, Guilt and Rejection by a significant Male Figure

High Cholesterol: <u>*Spirits:*</u> Self-Bitterness, Self-Hostility and Self-Anger

High Serotonin Problems: <u>*Spirits:*</u> Fear, Stress, Anxiety and Conflict. High Serotonin Problems include: Vomiting, Nausea, Aggressiveness, Violence, Migraine Headaches, and Bulimia Nervosa

High Triglycerides: <u>*Spirits:*</u> Self-Anger

Histamine Disorders: <u>*Spirits:*</u> Fear, Anxiety and Stress

Hives: <u>*Spirits:*</u> Fear, Stress and Anxiety

Hodgkin's Disease: <u>*Spirits:*</u> Deep-Rooted Bitterness from Unresolved Rejection, Abandonment by a Father either Literally or Emotionally, Resentment and Self-Hatred

Homosexuality: <u>*Spirits:*</u> Deaf and Dumb Spirit, Gender Disorientation, Double-Mindedness, Confusion, Rebellion, Occultism, Self-Rejection, Self-Hatred, Guilt and Spirit of Mistaken Identity

Hyperglycemia: <u>*Spirits:*</u> Extreme Rejection, Self-Hatred, Guilt, Rejection by a significant Male Figure (Father or Husband), Self-Rejection, Self-Hate, Self-Bitterness, Fear of Man and Hatred of Man

Hypertension: <u>*Spirits:*</u> Fear, Stress and Anxiety

Hyperventilation: *Spirits:* Fear, Anxiety and Stress

Hypoglycemia: *Spirits:* Fear, Anxiety, Stress, Self-Hatred Self-Rejection, Guilt and Performance

Hypothalamus Gland: *Spirits:* Fear, Stress, Anxiety, Rage Anger, Hostility, and Aggression.

Hypothyroidism: *Spirits:* Broken Relationship with God Others or Self, Fear, Stress, Anxiety, Self-Conflict and Unloving Spirit

Hypo-Thyroidism: *Spirits:* Fear, Stress, Anxiety and Broken Past Relationship

Hypothyroidism: *Spirits:* Long term Fear, Anxiety and Stress

CHAPTER 16 – I

IBS – Irritable Bowel Syndrome: *Spirits:* Worry, Double-Mindedness, Anger, Fear, Stress, Anxiety, Critical Spirit, and Insecurity.

IDF – Idiopathic Pulmonary Fibrosis: *Spirits:* Self-Hatred, Self-Guilt, Self-Rejection, Self-Bitterness, Self-Conflict, Fear, Stress and Anxiety. The person attacks themselves spiritually so the body attacks itself physically by sending white corpuscles to attack our body parts. Auto-immune

Idiopathic Pulmonary Fibrosis – IDF: *Spirits:* Self-Hatred, Self-Guilt, Self-Rejection, Self-Bitterness, Self-Conflict, Fear, Stress and Anxiety. The person attacks themselves spiritually so the body attacks itself physically sending white corpuscles to attack our body parts. Auto-immune

Idiopathic Thrombocytopenia Purpura – ITP: *Spirits:* Self-Hatred, Self-Guilt, Self-Rejection, Self-Bitterness, Self-Conflict, Fear, Anxiety and Stress. The person attacks themselves spiritually so the body attacks itself physically by sending white corpuscles to attack our body parts. Auto-immune

IgA Nephropathy: *Spirits:* Self-Hatred, Self-Guilt, Self-Rejection, Self-Bitterness, Self-Conflict, Fear, Stress and Anxiety. The person attacks themselves spiritually so the body attacks itself physically by sending white corpuscles to attack our body parts. Auto-immune

Immune System Disorder – ISD: *Spirits:* Fear, Anxiety, Stress and Broken Heart

Impatience: *Spirits:* Pride, Fear, Anxiety, Stress, and Selfishness

Impotence: *Spirits:* Fear, Anxiety, Stress, Uncleanness of Sexual Identity and Spirit of Diabetes

Inability to Concentrate: *Spirits:* Fear, Stress and Anxiety

Incontinence: *Spirits:* Fear, Stress, Anxiety, Self-Rejection, Lack of Self-Esteem, Worry, Double-Mindedness, Anger, Critical Spirit, and Insecurity.

Incurable Boils: *Spirits:* Bitterroot Judgments, Unforgiveness (towards Parents, Spouse, Ex-Spouse, Employers, Abusers, Molesters, etc.)

Incurable Itch: *Spirits:* Bitterroot Judgments, Unforgiveness (towards Parents, Spouse, Ex-Spouse, Employers, Abusers, Molesters, etc.)

Infertility: *Spirits:* Worry, Double-Mindedness, Anger, Fear, Stress, Anxiety, Critical Spirit, and Insecurity

Inflammation – Non-Bacterial: *Spirits:* Fear, Stress, Anxiety, Guilt and Self-Hatred

Inflammation: *Spirits:* Bitterroot Judgments, Unforgiveness (towards Parents, Spouse, Ex-Spouse, Employers, Abusers, Molesters, etc.)

Insanity: *Spirits:* Dumb and Deaf Spirit

Insecurity: *Spirits:* Fear, Stress, Anxiety and Not Trusting Yahovah

Insomnia: *Spirits:* Unresolved Conflict, Fear, Stress, Anxiety and Torment from Victimization, watching bloodshed and evil (Isaiah 33:13-16) (watching violent movies or TV shows), Worry, Double-Mindedness, Anger, Critical Spirit, and Insecurity.

Insulin Dependent Diabetes: *Spirits:* Self-Hatred, Self-Guilt, Self-Rejection, Self-Bitterness, Self-Conflict, Fear, Stress and Anxiety. The person attacks themselves spiritually so the body attacks itself physically by sending white corpuscles to attack our body parts. Auto-immune

Intercestral Cystitis: *Spirits:* Fear, Stress, Anxiety and Self-Rejection

Interstitial Cystitis: *Spirits:* Fear, Stress, Anxiety, Guilt and Self-Hatred

Intestine Disease: *Spirits:* Fear, Stress and Anxiety, Adultery, Abandonment, Rejection, Self-Rejection, Self-Bitterness, and Self-Hatred, Inherited Curse. Jealousy of a husband brings Curse on the wife.

Irregular Heartbeat: *Spirits:* Fear, Stress and Anxiety

Irregular Periods: *Spirits:* Worry, Double-Mindedness, Anger, Fear, Stress, Anxiety, Critical Spirit, and Insecurity.

Irritable Bowel Syndrome – IBS: *Spirits:* Fear, Stress, Anxiety, Worry, Double-Mindedness, Anger, Critical Spirit, Conflict and Insecurity

ISD – Immune System Disorder: *Spirits:* Broken Heart, Fear, Stress and Anxiety

Itching Skin: *Spirits:* Fear, Stress and Anxiety

ITP – Idiopathic Thrombocytopenia Purpura: *Spirits:* Self-Hatred, Self-Guilt, Self-Rejection, Self-Bitterness, Self-Conflict, Fear, Stress and Anxiety. The person attacks themselves spiritually so the body attacks itself physically by sending white corpuscles to attack our body parts. Auto-immune

Chapter 17 – J, K, L

Jealousy: _Spirits:_ Fear, Stress, Anxiety, Covetousness, Idolatry, Discontent, Envy, Unforgiveness, Resentment, Retaliation, Anger, Hatred, Violence, Murder, Bitterness, Criticalness, Competition, Gossip, Superiority, Inferiority, Strife, Possessiveness and Fear of Loss

Kidney Problems: _Spirits:_ Spirit of Dropsy.

Kleptomania: _Spirits:_ Lack of Proper Nurturing, Self-Hatred, Self-Rejection and Guilt

Leaky Gut Syndrome: _Spirits:_ Fear, Stress and Anxiety

Leg Problems: _Spirits:_ Adultery (Numbers 5:19-22) and Spirit of Loathsome.

Lethargy: _Spirits:_ Fear, Stress and Anxiety

Leukemia: _Spirits:_ Deep-Rooted Bitterness, Resentment, Self-Hatred, Unresolved Rejection and Abandonment (Literally or Emotionally) by a Father. There are 23 kinds of Leukemia. Each one could have a differing root.

Lichen Planus: _Spirits:_ Self-Hatred, Self-Guilt, Self-Conflict, Self-Rejection, Self-Bitterness, Fear, Stress and Anxiety. The person attacks themselves spiritually so the body attacks itself physically by sending white corpuscles to attack our body parts. Auto-immune

Liver Cancer: _Spirits:_ Fornication, Adultery, and Addiction to Pornography (Prov. 7:21-23) and Living a Lie

Liver Problems: *Spirits:* Spirit of Dropsy

Lou Gehrig's Disease: *Spirits:* Rejection, Self-Rejection, Self-Hatred, Heaviness, Oppression, Spirit and/or curse of Death, Hell and Destruction. Guilt, Fear, Stress and Anxiety if Biblar symptoms present.

Lou Gering's Disease – Biblar: *Spirits:* Guilt, Fear, Anxiety, Stress, Rejection from a father or significant male, Rejection, Self-Hatred

Low Blood Sugar – Hypoglycemia: *Spirits:* Fear, Stress, Anxiety, Self-Hatred, Self-Rejection and Performance

Low Serotonin Problems: *Spirits:* Lack of Proper Nurturing in Childhood, Self-Hatred, Self-Rejection and Guilt

Low Sperm Count: *Spirits:* Generational Violation of the laws of Niddah – Sexual Intercourse during a Period, Fornication, Pornography, Abortion, Sexual Affairs, Soul-Ties, Flashbacks of Past Relationships, Comparing Spouse with Parents, Oral Sex and Masturbation (a Homosexual act – Witchcraft).

Lower Back Pain: *Spirits:* Self-Bitterness, Unresolved Issues, Conflict with a Female (Mother, Sister, etc.), Self-Rejection, Self-Conflict, Spirit of Kundalini and Divination

Lupus – Discoid: *Spirits:* Self-Hatred, Self-Guilt, Self-Rejection, Self-Bitterness, Self-Conflict, Fear, Stress and Anxiety. The person attacks themselves spiritually so the body attacks itself physically by sending white corpuscles to attack our body parts. Auto-immune

Lupus: *Spirits:* Worry, Double-Mindedness, Anger, Critical Spirit, Insecurity, Condemnation, Guilt, Performance, Self-Hatred, Self-Guilt, Self-Rejection, Self-Bitterness, Self-Conflict, Fear, Stress and Anxiety. The person attacks themselves spiritually so the body attacks itself physically by sending white corpuscles to attack our body parts. Auto-immune

Lying: *Spirits:* Fear of Man, Fear of Rejection and Fear of Judgment

CHAPTER 18 – M

Malabsorption – Cell Wall Rigidity: *Spirits:* Fear, Stress and Anxiety

Malignant Tumor: *Spirits:* Bitterness against Others

Manic Depression: *Spirits:* Generational Fear, Stress and Anxiety. Spirit of Infirmity, False Religion, Occult, Witchcraft, SRA (Satanic Ritual Abuse), Ouiji Boards, etc., Male Victimization causes Manic Depression in Women. An inherited Genetic issue – ask Yahovah to reorder the 27th lower right-hand side of the X-Chromosome genetics to restore and repair the gene.

Manipulation: *Spirits:* Fear, Stress and Anxiety

Masturbation: *Spirits:* Guilt, Spirit of Homosexuality, Witchcraft, Incubus, Succubus and Spirit of Lust

MCS – Multiple Chemical Sensitivities: *Spirits:* Fear, Stress, Anxiety, Broken Heart, Occultism, Breakup in Relationship, Physical Abuse, Verbal Abuse, Sexual Abuse and Drivenness to meet expectations of the domineering cold Parent in order to receive their Love.

MCS/EI – Environmental Illness: *Spirits:* Fear, Stress, Anxiety, Broken Heart, Occultism, Breakup in Relationship, Physical Abuse, Verbal Abuse, Sexual Abuse and Drivenness to meet expectations of the domineering cold Parent in order to receive their Love.

MCTD – Mixed Connective Tissue Disease: *Spirits:* Self-Hatred, Self-Guilt, Self-Rejection, Self-Bitterness, Self-Conflict, Fear, Stress and Anxiety. The person attacks themselves spiritually so the body attacks itself physically by sending white corpuscles to attack our body parts. Auto-immune

Mega Doses of Vitamins: *Spirits:* Fear, Stress, Anxiety and Pharmakeia

Memory – Poor: *Spirits:* Spirit of Diabetes.

Ménière's Disease: *Spirits:* Self-Hatred, Self-Guilt, Self-Rejection, Self-Bitterness, Fear, Stress, Anxiety and Self-Conflict. The person attacks themselves spiritually so the body attacks itself physically by sending white corpuscles to attack our body parts. Auto-immune

Menstrual Cramps: *Spirits:* Generational Violation of the laws of Niddah – Sexual Intercourse during a Period, Fornication, Pornography, Abortion, Affairs, Soul-Ties, Flashbacks of Past Relationships, Comparing Spouse with parents, Oral Sex and Masturbation (a Homosexual Act – Witchcraft)

Mental Breakdowns: *Spirits:* Fear, Stress, Anxiety, Double-Mindedness, Occult, White Magic, Black Magic, Paganism, Earth Worship, Wicca, New Age, Secret Societies, Freemasonry, Lodges, Fraternities, Sororities, Horoscopes, Astrology, Ouija Boards, Tarot Cards, etc., and Spirit of Diabetes

Migraine Headache: *Spirits:* Fear, Stress, Anxiety, Conflict with Self, Self-Rejection, Self-Bitterness, Self-Hatred and

Guilt, Internalized Conflict, Inner Conflict over a Conflict with Another, Self-Hatred and Spirit of Diabetes

Migraine Headache – High Serotonin Problem: *Spirits:* Fear, Stress, Anxiety and Conflict

Mind Torment: *Spirits:* Spirits of Torment, Fear, Stress, Anxiety and Worry. Animal Spirits which can come from injections of animal origin.

Miscarriage: *Spirits:* Worry, Double-Mindedness, Anger, Fear, Stress, Anxiety, Critical Spirit, and Insecurity

Miscarriages – Multiple: *Spirits:* Fear, Stress, Anxiety, Self-Hatred and Guilt. Generational, Violation of the laws of Niddah – Sexual Intercourse during a Period, Fornication, Pornography, Abortion, Affairs, Soul-Ties, Flashbacks of Past Relationships, Comparing Spouse with Parents, Oral Sex and Masturbation (a Homosexual act – Witchcraft)

Missed Periods: *Spirits:* Worry, Double-Mindedness, Anger, Fear, Stress, Anxiety, Critical Spirit, and Insecurity

Mitral Valve Prolapse – MVP: *Spirits:* Fear, Stress and Anxiety

Mitral Valve Stenosis – MVS: *Spirits:* Worry, Double-Mindedness, Anger, Fear, Stress, Anxiety, Critical Spirit, and Insecurity

Mitro Valve Prolapse – Reflux: *Spirits:* Fear, Stress and Anxiety

Mitroval Prolac: *Spirits:* Fear, Stress and Anxiety

Mixed Connective Tissue Disease – MCTD: *Spirits:* Self-Hatred, Self-Guilt, Self-Rejection, Self-Bitterness, Fear, Stress, Anxiety and Self-Conflict. The person attacks themselves spiritually so the body attacks itself physically by sending white corpuscles to attack our body parts. Auto-immune

MPD – Multiple Personality Disorder: *Spirits:* Each Personality is an Evil Spirits that need to be cast out. The door is open through Satanic Ritual Abuse (SRA) or a trauma allowing entrance of Evil Spirits to "help" that person cope with the trauma.

MS – Multiple Sclerosis: *Spirits:* Self-Hatred, Self-Guilt, Self-Rejection, Self-Bitterness, Self-Conflict, Fear, Stress and Anxiety. The person attacks themselves spiritually so the body attacks itself physically by sending white corpuscles to attack our body parts. Auto-immune

Multiple Chemical Sensitivities – MCS: *Spirits:* Fear, Stress, Anxiety, Broken Heart and Occultism

Multiple Chemical Sensitivity – MCS: *Spirits:* Fear, Stress, Anxiety, Occult, Broken relationship, usually a close family member, Physical Abuse, Verbal Abuse, Sexual Abuse and Drivenness to meet expectations of the domineering cold parent attempting to receive their Love.

Multiple Miscarriages: *Spirits:* Fear, Stress, Anxiety, Self-Hatred, Guilt, Generational Violation of the laws of Niddah – Sexual Intercourse during a Period, Fornication, Pornography, Abortion, Affairs, Soul-Ties, Flashbacks of

Past Relationships, Comparing Spouse with Parents, Oral Sex and Masturbation (a Homosexual Act – Witchcraft)

Multiple Personality Disorder – MPD: *Spirits:* Each personality is an Evil Spirit that needs to be cast out. The door is open through Satanic Ritual Abuse (SRA) or a trauma which allows the evil spirits to enter to help that person deal with the trauma.

Multiple Sclerosis – MS: *Spirits:* Deep Self-Hatred, Shame, Guilt from a Father's rejection, Self-Guilt, Self-Rejection, Self-Bitterness, Fear, Stress, Anxiety and Self-Conflict. The person attacks themselves spiritually so the body attacks itself physically by sending white corpuscles to attack body parts. Sclerosis is one being eaten (auto-immune), multiple refers to many areas of attach, being eaten throughout the body. Nerves are also destroyed.

Muscle - Contractions: *Spirits:* Fear, Stress and Anxiety

MVP – Mitral Valve Prolapse: *Spirits:* Fear, Stress and Anxiety

MVS – Mitral Valve Stenosis: *Spirits:* Worry, Double-Mindedness, Anger, Fear, Stress, Anxiety, Critical Spirit, and Insecurity

Myasthenia Gravis: *Spirits:* Self-Hatred, Self-Guilt, Self-Rejection, Self-Bitterness, Fear, Stress, Anxiety and Self-Conflict. The person attacks themselves spiritually so the body attacks itself physically by sending white corpuscles to attack our body parts. Auto-immune

CHAPTER 19 – N, O

Nausea: *Spirits:* Fear, Stress and Anxiety

Nausea – High Serotonin Problem: *Spirits:* Fear, Stress, Anxiety and Conflict

Neck Problems: *Spirits:* Deaf and Dumb Spirit

Neckache: *Spirits:* Fear, Stress and Anxiety

Neurasthenia: *Spirits:* Fear, Stress and Anxiety

Neuro Dermatitis: *Spirits:* Fear, Stress and Anxiety

Neurofibromatosis: *Spirits:* Fear, Stress and Anxiety. Hereditary gene missing

No Strength: *Spirits:* Iniquity, Sadness (Prov 15:25), Lack of Trust in Yahovah

Non-Bacterial Inflammation: *Spirits:* Fear, Stress, Anxiety, Guilt and Self-Hatred

Non-Malignant Tumor: *Spirits:* Self-Bitterness

Nose – Runny: *Spirits:* Fear, Stress and Anxiety

Obesity: *Spirits:* Fear, Stress and Anxiety

Obsessive-Compulsive Disorder – OCD: *Spirits:* Lack of Self-Esteem, Lack of Proper Nurturing in Childhood, Self-Hatred, Self-Rejection, Guilt, Fear, Stress and Anxiety

OCD – Obsessive-Compulsive Disorder: *Spirits:* Lack of Self-Esteem, Lack of Proper Nurturing in childhood, Self-Hatred, Self-Rejection and Guilt

Organic Brain Syndrome: *Spirits:* Fear, Stress, Anxiety and Broken Relationship

Osteoarthritis: *Spirits:* Self-Bitterness, Unresolved Issues, Conflict with a Female (Mother), Self-Rejection, Spirit of Kundalini and Divination, Self-Hatred, Rejection, Guilt, Unresolved Issues, Conflict with another female (mother), Self-Rejection and Self-Conflict, Spirit of Kundalini and Divination when injury is not present.

Osteoarthritis Spondilyosis: *Not a Spirit:* Result of injury to compromised tissue

Osteoporosis: *Spirits:* Bitterness, Envy, Control, Matriarchal Witchcraft and Jealousy. Worry, Double-Mindedness, Anger, Fear, Stress, Anxiety, Critical Spirit and Insecurity.

Ovarian Cancer: *Spirits:* Self-Bitterness, Self-Hatred regarding one's own sexuality and Promiscuity

Ovarian Cysts: *Spirits:* Conflict with the mother. Unresolved Bitterness between a woman and a close Female Figure (Mother or Sister), Generational Violation of the laws of Niddah – Sexual Intercourse during a Period, Fornication, Pornography, Abortion, Affairs, Soul-Ties, Flashbacks of Past Relationships, Comparing Spouse with Parents, Oral Sex and Masturbation (a Homosexual act – Witchcraft)

Overeating: *Spirits:* Fear of Rejection, Fear of Man, Fear of Failure, Fear of Abandonment, Self-Hatred, Self-Rejection and Guilt

Overweight: *Spirits:* Lack of Self-Esteem, Self-Conflict, Fear of Man, Fear of Failure, Fear of Abandonment, Fear of Rejection, Introspection, Manipulation, Control and Stress

CHAPTER 20 – P

Palsy: *Spirits:* Spirit of Palsy and Spirit of Candor

Pancreas Cancer: *Spirits:* Self- Bitterness, Self-Hatred, Self- Rejection, Fear, Stress, Anxiety, Spirit of Pancreatic Cancer and Generational Familiar Spirits. This disease is diagnosed in early stages as Diabetes.

Panic Attacks: *Spirits:* Worry, Double-Mindedness, Anger, Fear, Stress, Anxiety, Critical Spirit, and Insecurity

Panic Disorder: *Spirits:* Fear, Stress and Anxiety

Paranoia: *Spirits:* Mirrors Manic Depression. All Self-Spirits

Paranoid Schizophrenia: *Spirits:* Fear, Stress, Anxiety, Rejection and Rebellion

Parasites: *Spirits:* Long term Fear, Stress and Anxiety

Parkinson's Disease: *Spirits:* Worry, Double-Mindedness, Anger, Critical Spirit, Insecurity, Fear, Stress, Anxiety, Broken Relationship with Parent or Guardian, Broken Relationship with Father or Male Figure, Drivenness to meet Expectations of a Parent to receive Love and Acceptance, Abandonment, Rejection, Hope Deferred, Loss of Hope, Broken Spirit, Self-Hatred, Failure, Spirit of Mistaken Identity, Hopelessness, Bitterness, Self-Guilt, Self-Conflict and Expectations Unfulfilled

PDD – Premenstrual Dysphoric Disorder: *Spirits:* Lack of Proper Nurturing in Childhood, Self-Hatred, Self-Rejection and Guilt

Pemphigus Vulgaris: *Spirits:* Fear, Stress, Anxiety, Self-Hatred, Self-Guilt, Self-Rejection, Self-Bitterness and Self-Conflict. The person attacks themselves spiritually so the body attacks itself physically by sending white corpuscles to attack our body parts. Auto-immune

Perfectionism: *Spirits:* Fear, Stress and Anxiety

Performance Disorder: *Spirits:* Fear, Stress, Anxiety and Need to Succeed to be Loved or Feel Whole

Pernicious Anemia: *Spirits:* Fear, Stress, Anxiety, Self-Hatred, Self-Guilt, Self-Rejection, Self-Bitterness and Self-Conflict. The person attacks themselves spiritually so the body attacks itself physically by sending white corpuscles to attack our body parts. Auto-immune

Phenylketonuria: *Spirits:* Fear, Stress and Anxiety

Phobias – Agoraphobia: *Spirit Family Notes:* Fear of having Severe Anxiety or Panic Attack in a place or situation where escape may be difficult or embarrassing. Starts about age 29.

Phobias – General: *Spirits:* Fear, Stress and Anxiety

Phobias – Social Phobia: *Spirits:* Extreme Fear of feeling embarrassed, humiliated or scorned in public. Starts between the ages of 15 and 16

Phobias – Specific Phobia: *Spirits:* Extreme Fear of a specific object or situation that is not harmful under usual conditions. Starts between the ages of 15 and 16

Pinched Nerve: *Spirits:* Not a spiritual problem. You need to ask Yahovah to release that nerve.

Plague: *Spirits:* Bitterroot Judgments, Unforgiveness (towards Parents, Spouse, Ex-Spouse, Employers, Abusers, Molesters, etc.)

PMS: *Spirits:* Lack of Proper Nurturing in Childhood, Self-Hatred, Self-Rejection and Guilt.

Polyarteritis Nodosa: *Spirits:* Self-Hatred, Self-Guilt, Self-Rejection, Self-Bitterness, Fear, Stress, Anxiety and Self-Conflict. The person attacks themselves spiritually so the body attacks itself physically by sending white corpuscles to attack our body parts. Auto-immune

Polychondritis: *Spirits:* Fear, Stress, Anxiety, Self-Hatred, Self-Guilt, Self-Rejection, Self-Bitterness, and Self-Conflict. The person attacks themselves spiritually so the body attacks itself physically by sending white corpuscles to attack our body parts. Auto-immune

Polyglandular Syndromes: *Spirits:* Fear, Stress, Anxiety, Self-Hatred, Self-Guilt, Self-Rejection, Self-Bitterness and Self-Conflict. The person attacks themselves spiritually so the body attacks itself physically by sending white corpuscles to attack our body parts. Auto-immune

Polymyalgia Rheumatica: *Spirits:* Fear, Stress, Anxiety, Self-Hatred, Self-Guilt, Self-Rejection, Self-Bitterness and

Self-Conflict. The person attacks themselves spiritually so the body attacks itself physically by sending white corpuscles to attack our body parts. Auto-immune

Polymyositis: *Spirits:* Fear, Stress, Anxiety, Self-Hatred, Self-Guilt, Self-Rejection, Self-Bitterness and Self-Conflict. The person attacks themselves spiritually so the body attacks itself physically by sending white corpuscles to attack our body parts. Auto-immune

Poor Memory: *Spirits:* Spirit of Diabetes

Postpartum Depression: *Spirits:* Worry, Double-Mindedness, Anger, Fear, Stress, Anxiety, Critical Spirit, and Insecurity.

Postpartum Disorders: *Spirits:* Fear, Stress and Anxiety

Post-Traumatic Stress Disorder – PTSD: *Spirits:* Worry, Double-Mindedness, Anger, Fear, Stress, Anxiety, Critical Spirit, and Insecurity

Pregnancy – Problems: *Spirits:* Spirit of Diabetes, Fear, Stress and Anxiety

Pregnancy Discomforts: *Spirits:* Worry, Double-Mindedness, Anger, Fear, Stress, Anxiety, Critical Spirit, and Insecurity

Premenstrual Dysphoric Disorder – PDD: *Spirits:* Lack of Proper Nurturing in Childhood, Self-Hatred, Self-Rejection and Guilt

Premenstrual Syndrome: *Spirits:* Fear, Stress, Anxiety and Not accepting one's Femaleness

Primary Agammag-lobulinemia: *Spirits:* Fear, Stress, Anxiety, Self-Hatred, Self-Guilt, Self-Rejection, Self-Bitterness and Self-Conflict. The person attacks themselves spiritually so the body attacks itself physically by sending white corpuscles to attack our body parts. Auto-immune

Primary Biliary Cirrhosis: *Spirits:* Fear, Stress, Anxiety, Self-Hatred, Self-Guilt, Self-Rejection, Self-Bitterness and Self-Conflict. The person attacks themselves spiritually so the body attacks itself physically by sending white corpuscles to attack our body parts. Auto-immune

Programming – Cult: – *Spirits:* Fear, Stress, Anxiety, Bondage, Accusation, Recorder, Abuse, Slander, Self-Bitterness, Self-Unforgiveness, Self-Resentment, Self-Retaliation, Self-Anger/Self-Wrath, Self-Hate, Self-Violence, Self-Murder

Programming – Spousal: – *Spirits:* Fear, Stress, Anxiety, Bondage, Accusation, Recorder, Abuse, Slander, Self-Bitterness, Self-Unforgiveness, Self-Resentment, Self-Retaliation, Self-Anger/Self-Wrath, Self-Hate, Self-Violence, Self-Murder

Promiscuity: *Spirits:* Need to be Loved, Lack of Self-Esteem, Self-Hatred and Bastard's Curse

Prostate Cancer: *Spirits:* Anger, Guilt, Self-Hatred, Self-Bitterness, Self-Conflict with being a Man, and Self-Rejection, Promiscuity, Self-Hatred at being a Male, Not accepting one's Maleness, Generational Violation of the laws of Niddah – Sexual Intercourse during a Period, Fornication, Pornography, Abortion, Affairs, Soul-Ties,

Flashbacks of Past Relationships, Comparing Spouse with parents, Oral Sex and Masturbation (a Homosexual Act – Witchcraft).

Prostatitus: *Spirits:* Fear, Stress, Anxiety and Self-Rejection cause the cells to congregate in your body producing Non-Bacterial Inflammation

Psoriasis: *Spirits:* Worry, Double-Mindedness, Anger, Critical Spirit, Insecurity, Fear, Stress, Anxiety, Self-Hatred, Lack of Self-Esteem, Conflict with one's own identity and Rejection

Psoriasis – Raynaud's Phenomenon: *Spirits:* Fear, Stress, Anxiety, Self-Hatred, Self-Guilt, Self-Rejection, Self-Bitterness and Self-Conflict. The person attacks themselves spiritually so the body attacks itself physically by sending white corpuscles to attack our body parts. Auto-immune

Psoriatic Arthritis: *Spirits:* Worry, Double-Mindedness, Anger, Fear, Stress, Anxiety, Critical Spirit, and Insecurity

PTSD – Post-Traumatic Stress Disorder: *Spirits:* Worry, Double-Mindedness, Anger, Fear, Stress, Anxiety, Critical Spirit, and Insecurity

CHAPTER 21 – R

Rashes: *Spirits:* Spirits: Fear, Anxiety and Stress

Raynaud's Phenomenon – Psoriasis: *Spirits:* Fear, Stress, Anxiety, Self-Hatred, Self-Guilt, Self-Rejection, Self-Bitterness and Self-Conflict. The person attacks themselves spiritually so the body attacks itself physically by sending white corpuscles to attack our body parts. Auto-immune

Reflux: *Spirits:* Fear, Stress and Anxiety

Reflux – Heartburn: *Spirits:* Fear, Stress and Anxiety

Reflux – Mitro Valve Prolapse: *Spirits:* Fear, Stress and Anxiety

Reiter's Syndrome: *Spirits:* Fear, Stress, Anxiety, Self-Hatred, Self-Guilt, Self-Rejection, Self-Bitterness and Self-Conflict. The person attacks themselves spiritually so the body attacks itself physically by sending white corpuscles to attack our body parts. Auto-immune

Retaliation: *Spirits:* Unloving Spirit and Spirit of Death. Part of the Bitterness Kingdom

Retention of Toxins: *Spirits:* Fear, Stress, Anxiety and Broken Relationship

Rheumatic Fever: *Spirits:* Fear, Stress, Anxiety, Self-Hatred, Self-Guilt, Self-Rejection, Self-Bitterness and Self-Conflict. The person attacks themselves spiritually so the body attacks itself physically by sending white corpuscles to attack our body parts. Auto-immune

Rheumatoid Arthritis: *Spirits:* Bitterness and Unforgiveness toward another, dead or alive, Self-Rejection, Self-Hate, Guilt, Self-Guilt, Self-Conflict, Self-Rejection, Fear, Stress, Anxiety and Self-Bitterness. The person attacks themselves spiritually so the body attacks itself physically by sending white corpuscles to attack our body parts. Auto-imune

Ringing In Ears: *Spirits:* Damage from drug overdose, accident or loud noise opens the door to a spirit of Witchcraft and Occult

Rosacea: *Spirits:* Self-Hatred

Runny Nose: *Spirits:* Fear, Stress and AnxietyC

CHAPTER 22 – S

Sadness: *Spirits:* Fear, Stress, Anxiety, Unforgiveness, Hope Deferred and Broken Relationship

Sarcoidosis: *Spirits:* Fear, Stress, Anxiety, Self-Hatred, Self Guilt, Self-Rejection, Self-Bitterness and Self-Conflict. The person attacks themselves spiritually so the body attacks itself physically by sending white corpuscles to attack our body parts. Auto-immune

Scabs: *Spirits:* Bitterroot Judgments, Unforgiveness (towards Parents, Spouse, Ex-Spouse, Employers, Abusers Molesters, etc.)

Schizophrenia: *Spirits:* Fear, Stress, Anxiety, Conflict from Confused Relationship with Family Members (a Parent says one thing and does another), Self-Rejection, Self-Guilt and Bitterness

Sciatica: *Spirits:* Self-Bitterness, Unresolved Issues Conflict with Female (Mother), Self-Rejection, Self-Conflict, Spirit of Kundalini, Divination, Spirit of Sciatica, Self-Hatred and Unresolved Issues when injury is not present.

Scleroderma: *Spirits:* Fear, Stress, Anxiety, Spirits: Self-Hatred, Guilt, Self-Guilt, Self-Rejection, Self-Bitterness and Self-Conflict. The person attacks themselves spiritually so the body attacks itself physically by sending white corpuscles to attack our body parts. Auto-immune

Scoliosis: *Spirits:* Self-Bitterness, Unresolved Issues, Conflict with another Female (Mother), Self-Rejection and

Self-Conflict, Spirit of Scoliosis, Spirit of Kundalini and Divination when injury is not present. Command the spine to straighten and atrophied muscles to be restored

Seizures – Various Types: *Spirits:* Deaf and Dumb Spirit and Unclean Spirit

Selective Mutism: *Spirits:* Fear, Stress and Anxiety.

Serotonin Deficiency: *Spirits:* Self-Hatred, Self-Bitterness, Deaf and Dumb Spirit, Gender Disorientation, Double-Mindedness, Confusion; Rebellion, Occultism, Self-Rejection, Self-Hatred, and Guilt

Severe Burning/Fever: *Spirits:* Bitterroot Judgments and Unforgiveness (towards Parents, Spouse, Ex-Spouse, Employers, Abusers, Molesters, etc.)

Shell Shock Syndrome: *Spirits:* Worry, Double-Mindedness, Anger, Fear, Stress, Anxiety, Critical Spirit, and Insecurity

Shingles: *Spirits:* Fear, Stress, Anxiety and Self-Rejection

Shop Lifting: *Spirits:* Lack of Proper Nurturing in Childhood, Self-Hatred, Self-Rejection and Guilt

Shutting Down – Panic Attacks: *Spirits:* Fear, Stress and Anxiety

Sickle Cell Disease: *Spirits:* Worry, Double-Mindedness, Anger, Fear, Stress, Anxiety, Critical Spirit, and Insecurity

Simple Arthritis: *Spirits:* Bitterness against others

Sinus Infection – Chronic: *Spirits:* Fear, Stress and Anxiety

Sinusitis: *Spirits:* Fear, Stress and Anxiety

Sjögren's Syndrome: *Spirits:* Guilt, Self-Hatred, Self-Guilt, Self-Rejection, Self-Bitterness, Fear, Stress, Anxiety and Self-Conflict. The person attacks themselves spiritually so the body attacks itself physically by sending white corpuscles to attack our body parts. Auto-immune

Skin – Flaking: *Spirits:* Fear, Stress, Anxiety, Self-Hatred, Lack of Self-Esteem, Conflict with one's own Identity, and Rejection.

Skin – Hardness: *Spirits:* Fear, Stress, Anxiety, Self-Hatred, Lack of Self-Esteem, Conflict with one's own Identity, and Rejection.

Skin – Itching: *Spirits:* Fear, Stress and Anxiety

Skin – Rashes: *Spirits:* Fear, Stress and Anxiety

Skin – Redness: *Spirits:* Fear, Stress, Anxiety, Self-Hatred, Lack of Self-Esteem, Conflict with one's own Identity, and Rejection.

Skin – Scaling: *Spirits:* Fear, Stress, Anxiety, Self-Hatred, Lack of Self-Esteem, Conflict with one's own Identity, and Rejection.

Skin Cancer: *Spirits:* Inherited Long-term Bitterness, Hatred, Anger, Retaliation, Helplessness, Broken Relationship with Yahovah, Self or Others. Can be caused by not protecting the skin from the sun.

SLE – Systematic Lupus Erythematosus: <u>*Spirits:*</u> Worry, Double-Mindedness, Anger, Fear, Stress, Anxiety, Critical Spirit, and Insecurity

Sleep Apnea: <u>*Spirits:*</u> Conflict, Deaf and Dumb Spirit, Depression, Occultism and False Religion

Sleep Disorders: <u>*Spirits:*</u> Fear, Stress, Anxiety, Torment from Victimization, Not stopping your eyes from the hearing of blood and shutting your eyes from the seeing of evil (Isaiah 33:13-16), watching violent movies or TV shows. (Proverbs 3:21-24), Worry, Double-Mindedness, Anger, Critical Spirit, and Insecurity

Slipped Disc: <u>*Spirits:*</u> Self-Bitterness, Unresolved Issues, Conflict with another Female (Mother), Self-Rejection, Self-Conflict, Spirit of Kundalini and Divination when injury is not present

Spending – Uncontrolled: <u>*Spirits:*</u> Adulterous Affairs, Pornography, Greed, Sexual Immorality, Spirit of Lust, Anger and Rage.

Sperm Count – Low: <u>*Spirits:*</u> Generational Violation of the laws of Niddah – Sexual Intercourse during a Period. Fornication, Pornography, Abortion, Affairs, Soul-Ties, Flashbacks of Past Relationships, Comparing Spouse with Parents, Oral Sex and Masturbation (a Homosexual act – Witchcraft)

Spondilyosis – Osteoarthritis: <u>*Not a Spirit:*</u> Result of injury to possibly compromised tissue

Spondylolyosis: *Spirits:* Self-Hatred, Self-Bitterness, Unresolved Issues, Conflict with another Female (Mother), Self-Rejection, Self-Conflict, Spirit of Kundalini and Divination when injury is not present

Spondylosis: *Spirits:* Self-Bitterness, Unresolved Issues, Conflict with another Female (Mother), Self-Rejection, Self-Conflict, Spirit of Kundalini and Divination

STDs – Transmission: *Spirits:* Generational Violation of the laws of Niddah – Sexual Intercourse during a Period. Fornication, Pornography, Abortion, Affairs, Soul-Ties, Flashbacks of Past Relationships, Comparing Spouse with Parents, Oral Sex and Masturbation (a Homosexual act – Witchcraft)

Stiff-Man Syndrome: *Spirits:* Self-Hatred, Self-Guilt, Self-Rejection, Self-Bitterness, Stress, Anxiety, Self-Conflict and Fear. The person attacks themselves spiritually so the body attacks itself physically by sending white corpuscles to attack our body parts. Auto-immune

Stomach Problems: *Spirits:* Adultery (Num 5:19-22), Spirit of Convulsions, Spirit of Loathsome, Fear, Stress, Anxiety, Anger, Guilt, Hopelessness, Disparity, Fear of Future, Self-Rejection. Divination and Kundalini (the snake is wrapped around the lower back/stomach area and sometimes causes stomach problems)

Strength Gone: *Spirits:* Grief, Complaining, Self-Pity, What-About-Me, Disgust, and Dissatisfaction

Stress Disorders: *Spirits:* Worry, Double-Mindedness, Anger, Fear, Stress, Anxiety, Critical Spirit, and Insecurity

Stroke: *Spirits:* Fear, Stress, Anxiety, Unresolved Anger, great Bitterness, Worry, Double-Mindedness, Critical Spirit, Insecurity, Anger, Rage and Resentment, Unresolved Rage, Anger, Spirit of Stroke, Hostility and Bitterness

Sty: *Spirits:* Fear, Stress and Anxiety

Suicide: *Spirits:* Self-Bitterness, Self-Murder and Spirit of Death

Systematic Lupus Erythematosus – SLE: *Spirits:* Worry, Double-Mindedness, Anger, Fear, Stress, Anxiety, Critical Spirit and Insecurity

Systolic Acne: *Spirits:* Unresolved Bitterness, Conflict between a Woman and a close Female Figure (Mother, Sister, Mother-in-law). Forgive the female in question

CHAPTER 23 – T

Takayasu Arteritis: *Spirits:* Fear, Stress, Anxiety, Self Hatred, Self-Guilt, Self-Rejection, Self-Bitterness and Self Conflict. The person attacks themselves spiritually so the body attacks itself physically by sending white corpuscles to attack our body parts. Auto-immune

TB: *Spirits:* This is an infection: Fear, Stress, Anxiety and Spirit of Infirmity makes one vulnerable to infection

Temporal Arteritis: *Spirits:* Fear, Stress, Anxiety, Self Hatred, Self-Guilt, Self-Rejection, Self-Bitterness and Self Conflict. The person attacks themselves spiritually so the body attacks itself physically by sending white corpuscles to attack our body parts. Auto-immune

Temporomandibular Disorder – TMJ: *Spirits:* Worry Double-Mindedness, Anger, Fear, Stress, Anxiety, Critical Spirit, and Insecurity.

Tension Headache: *Spirits:* Fear, Stress, Anxiety, Self-Hatred, Self-Rejection, Guilt, Spirit of Diabetes, Lack of Proper Nurturing in Childhood, Worry, Double-Mindedness, Anger, Critical Spirit and Insecurity.

Thigh Disease: *Spirits:* Fear, Stress, Anxiety, Abandonment, Rejection, Self-Rejection, Self-Bitterness, Self-Hatred, Inherited Curse and Adultery. Jealousy of a husband brings Curse on the wife.

Throat Cancer: *Spirits:* Broken Spirit, Unforgiveness, Unresolved Conflict with Others and Self, Fear, Stress and Anxiety.

Thromophlebitis: *Spirits:* Anger, Rage and Resentment

Tinnitus: *Spirits:* Fear, Stress, Anxiety, Self-Hatred and Guilt

TMJ – Temporomandibular Disorder: *Spirits:* Worry, Double-Mindedness, Anger, Fear, Stress, Anxiety, Critical Spirit, and Insecurity

Too Low Cholesterol: *Spirits:* Lack of Proper Nurturing in Childhood, Self-Hatred, Self-Rejection and Guilt

Tourette's Syndrome: *Spirits:* Worry, Double-Mindedness, Anger, Fear, Stress, Anxiety, Critical Spirit, and Insecurity

Toxic Retention: *Spirits:* Fear, Stress and Anxiety

Triglycerides – High: *Spirits:* Self-Anger

Tuberculosis: *Spirits:* This is an infection. Fear, Stress, Anxiety, Spirit of Infirmity cause vulnerability to infection

Tumor – Malignant: *Spirits:* Bitterness against others

Tumor – Non-Malignant: *Spirits:* Self-Bitterness

Tumor: *Spirits:* Bitterroot Judgments, Unforgiveness (towards Parents, Spouse, Ex-Spouse, Employers, Abusers, Molesters, etc.)

Type A Behavior: *Spirits:* Fear of Poverty, Need to Succeed to be Loved, Expectation put on by a Parent or Spouse, Drivenness, Performance and Perfectionism

CHAPTER 24 – U, V, W

Ulcers: *Spirits:* Fear, Stress and Anxiety allowing H-pylori bacteria to proliferate

Ulcerative Colitis: *Spirits:* Fear, Stress, Anxiety, Unresolved Conflict, Self-Hatred, Self-Guilt, Self-Rejection, Self-Bitterness and Self-Conflict. The person attacks themselves spiritually so the body attacks itself physically by sending white corpuscles to attack our body parts. Auto-immune

Uncontrolled Spending: *Spirits:* Adulterous Affairs, Pornography, Greed, Sexual Immorality, Spirit of Lust, Anger and Rage.

Unforgiveness: *Spirits:* Unloving Spirit and Spirit of Death. Part of the Bitterness Kingdom

Uterine Cancer: *Spirits:* Need to be Loved, Promiscuity, Uncleanness, Self-Conflict with being a Man, Self-Rejection and Self-Hatred

Uveitis: *Spirits:* Self-Hatred, Self-Guilt, Self-Rejection, Self-Bitterness, Self-Conflict and Fear. The person attacks themselves spiritually so the body attacks itself physically by sending white corpuscles to attack our body parts. Auto-immune

Vaginitis: *Spirits:* Fear, Stress, Anxiety and Broken Relationship

Varicose Veins: *Spirits:* Fear, Stress, Anxiety, Anger, Rage, Resentment, Unresolved Rage, Spirit of Stroke, Hostility, Bitterness, Unresolved Anger, and great Bitterness

Vasculitis: *Spirits:* Self-Hatred, Self-Guilt, Self-Rejection, Self-Bitterness, Fear, Stress, Anxiety and Self-Conflict. The person attacks themselves spiritually so the body attacks itself physically by sending white corpuscles to attack our body parts. Auto-immune

Vein Inflammation: *Spirits:* Anger, Rage and Resentment

Vertigo: *Spirits:* Fear, Stress, Anxiety, Self-Hatred and Guilt

Violence – High Serotonin Problem: *Spirits:* Fear, Stress, Anxiety and Conflict

Violence: *Spirits:* Lack of Proper Nurturing in Childhood, Self-Hatred, Self-Rejection and Guilt

Virus: *Spirits:* Spirit of Infirmity, Fear, Stress and Anxiety

Vitiligo: *Spirits:* Fear, Stress, Anxiety, Self-Hatred, Self-Guilt, Self-Rejection, Self-Bitterness and Self-Conflict. The person attacks themselves spiritually so the body attacks itself physically by sending white corpuscles to attack our body parts. Auto-immune

Vomiting: *Spirits:* Fear, Stress and Anxiety

Vomiting – High Serotonin Problem: *Spirits:* Fear, Stress, Anxiety and Conflict

Wasting Diseases: *Spirits:* Bitterroot Judgments and Unforgiveness (towards Parents, Spouse, Ex-Spouse, Employers, Abusers, Molesters, etc.)

WCDB – White Corpuscle Deviate Behavior: *Spirits:* Fear, Stress, Anxiety and Self-Rejection

Weakness: *Spirits:* Grief, Complaining, Self-Pity, What-About-Me, Disgust, and Dissatisfaction

Wegener's Granulomatosis: *Spirits:* Fear, Stress, Anxiety, Self-Hatred, Self-Guilt, Self-Rejection, Self-Bitterness and Self-Conflict. The person attacks themselves spiritually so the body attacks itself physically by sending white corpuscles to attack our body parts. Auto-immune

Weight Gain: *Spirits:* Worry, Double-Mindedness, Anger, Fear, Stress, Anxiety, Critical Spirit, and Insecurity.

Weight Problems: *Spirits:* Lack of Proper Nurturing in Child hood, Lack of Self-Esteem, Self-Conflict, Fear of Man, Fear of Failure, Fear of Abandonment and Fear of Rejection

White Corpuscle Deviate Behavior – WCDB: *Spirits:* Fear, Stress, Anxiety and Self-Rejection

Winter Blues: *Spirits:* Lack of Proper Nurturing in Childhood, Self-Hatred, Self-Rejection and Guilt

Workaholic: *Spirits:* Fear of Poverty, Need to Succeed to be Loved, Expectation put on someone by a Parent or Spouse, Drivenness, Performance and Perfectionism

Worms (Parasites): *Spirits:* (Mark 9:45-50) Parasites = Sin.

Chapter 25 – Spirits and Spirit Families

Spirits work in families with common assignments. Below is a list of Spirit Families who work together or with similar assignments.

Absalom: *Spirits:* Pride, Vanity, Rebellion, Deception, Seduction, Treachery: Mind Idolatry, Vanity, Perfection, Competition, Schizophrenia, Self-Righteousness, Haughtiness, Importance, Arrogance, Self-Deception and Ego

Addictions: *Spirits:* Excessive Spending, Self-Destruction, Mask Pain, Obesity, Overweight, Love For Food, Gluttony, Overeating, I'm Fat Spirit, Escapism, Fear, Anger, Bitterness, Suicide, Masochism, Sadism, Pain, Loneliness, Emptiness, Self-Hate, Self-Bitterness, Lack of Self-Esteem, Lack of Discipline, etc.

Addictive Behavior Spirits: *Spirits:* Addiction (including intense sports, drugs, alcohol, shopping, etc.), Drug Personality, Need to be Loved, Lack of Self-Esteem, Insecurity, Lack of Proper Nurturing, Generational Sins (be specific if known), Desperation and Unbalanced Need.

Additimus: *Spirits:* Additimus blocks Spiritual Truth

Ahab Spirits: *Spirits:* Abdicating Leadership, Adultery, Aggression, Avoiding Work, Bitterness, Blaming Others, Blaming Wife, Carelessness, Childish Behavior, Communication Breakdown, Compromise, Conditional

Love, Conflict, Considering Torah Trivial, Covetousness, Degradation, Destruction of Family Priesthood, Disobedient, Don't Want To Work, Effeminate, Emasculation, Emotional Cripple, Failure, Fear of Getting Hurt, Fear of Women, Following Sins of the Father, Foolishness, Homosexuality, Hurts, Idol Worship, Impotence, Inability to Designate Authority, Indecision, Irresponsibility, Lack Of Authority, Lack Of Character, Lack of Confidence, Laziness, Leaning On Others, Little Boy, Lust of Material Things, Lust Sensual Women, Mama's Boy, No Order, No Peace, No Unity, Passive Quitter, Passivity, Rejection, Resentment, Scared, Sibling Rivalry, Sluggishness, Temper Tantrums, Undependability, Unreliability, Weakness and Insecurity

Anger/Self-Wrath: *Spirits:* Unloving Spirit, Spirit of Death, Part of the Bitterness Kingdom (see below)

Anti-Messiah: *Spirits:* Inability to Love, Religious Spirit, Covetousness, Idolatry, Discontent, Jealousy, Unforgiveness, Resentment, Retaliation, Anger, Hatred, Violence, Murder, Bitterness, Competition, Gossip, Superiority, Strife, Possessiveness, Fear of Loss, Self-Idolatry, Self-Pride, Selfishness, I and I Will, Self-Exaltation, Prefabricated Personality, Self-Pity, Rebellion, Self-Deception, Deception, Division, Separation and Generational Familiar Spirits. The assignment of Anti-Messiah is to trash self and others.

Argumentative: (James 3:16) Where Strife is every evil thing resides

The Spiritual Roots of Common Diseases

Bitterness Kingdom: *Spirits:* Unforgiveness, Resentment, Retaliation, Anger, Wrath, Hate, Violence and Murder.

Black Prejudice Kingdom: *Spirits:* Down Playing Heritage, Hatred Of African Features (Color and Features), Black Hatred, Hatred For Whites, Black Pride, African Pride, Theft, Dehumanization, Pain, Brutality, Betrayal, Fear, Shame, Helplessness, Bitterness, Self-Hatred, Oppression, Lack Of Inheritance, Poverty, Occult, Pagan gods, JuJu, Etc.

Carbar: *Spirits:* Carbar is a Ruler or Principality who Blocks Spiritual Truth

Carvar: Carvar is a spirit who leads victims to Spiritual Destruction and Under Spirit Of Lucifer

Competition: *Spirits:* Pride, Driving, Argument, Ego, Compromise, Indecision, Blocked Spiritual Growth and Orion

Controlling: The root of a controlling personality is Fear, Stress, Anxiety and Witchcraft

Dark Interaction: *Spirits:* Distrust, Meanness, Spitefulness, Physical Abuse, Unfaithfulness, Control, Disobedience, Adultery, Fornication, Addiction, Murder, Hate, Occult, False Religion, Anti-Torahism, Torahlessness, Eastern Star, Islam, Hypocrisy And Masonry, etc.

Death: *Spirits:* Death, Destruction, Abaddon, Apollyon, Suicide, Abortion, Murder, Crimes and Early Death, etc.

Demonic Tongues: *Spirits:* Flattering, Smooth Talker, Slandering, Deceitfulness, Sharpness, Pride, Lying,

Falsehoods, Backbiting, Stammering, Craftiness, Confusion, Striving, Mischief, Full Of Adder's Poison, Frowardness, Naughty, Perverse, Evil Fire, Double-Mindedness, Trouble, Sin, Iniquity, etc.

Drivenness: The need to perform to gain recognition, attention, love and acceptance. Drivenness is built on the fear of being rejected and/or the fear of not being in control. It works with Manipulation which promotes an Unloving Spirit and Fear in others.

Ego: *Spirits:* Mind Idolatry, Pride, Perfection, Competition and Schizophrenia

Envy: *Spirits:* Fear, Stress, Anxiety, Covetousness, Idolatry, Discontent, Jealousy, Unforgiveness, Resentment, Retaliation, Anger, Hatred, Violence, Murder, Bitterness, Criticalness, Competition, Gossip, Superiority, Inferiority, Strife, Possessiveness and Fear of Loss

Fear: Genesis 3:10 Fear comes by disobedience. (2 Tim 1:7) Yahovah has not given us a spirit of fear but power, love and a sound mind. Fear is a tool of HaSatan, Lucifer the devil, to force us to eventually curse ourselves and sin in desperation.

Grief: *Spirits:* Grief, Torment, Sorrow, Sadness, Hardship, Affliction, Burden Bearing and Oppression

Hatred: *Spirits:* Unloving and Spirit of Death. Part of the Bitterness Kingdom.

Hopelessness: *Spirits:* This comes from not knowing one's real identity in Yahovah. Spiritual Root is Doubt, Fear,

Stress, Anxiety, Unbelief and Mistaken Identity. Hopelessness can manifest as Parkinson's Disease.

Idolatry: Putting anything before Yahovah including self, idols, movie stars, sport stars, doctors, gurus, authority figures, etc.

Immorality Spirits: *Spirits:* Abortion, Adultery and Blasphemy

Infirmity: *Spirits:* Infirmity, High Blood Pressure, Heart Disease, Arthritis, Lupus, Cancer, Stroke, Hardening Of Arteries, Mental Illness, Worry, Pandemonium, Anxiety, Pharmakeia, etc.

Inherited Disease: Sin will rewrite and rearrange our genetic DNA code over the centuries which is passed on by Familiar Spirits and genetic code through Family lines.

Jezebel Demons: *Spirits:* Accusation, Adultery, Aggression, Altercation, Arguing, Arrogance, Attention Seeking, Authoritarian, Backbiting, Beguiling, Belittling, Bickering, Brash, Center of Attention, Charming, Competitive, Conceit, Condemnation, Conditional Love, Conflict, Confusion, Conniving, Contention, Complaining, Control, Covetousness, Critical Spirit, Curses, Deception, Defiance, Delusion, Despising Husband, Discontent, Disobedience, Dispute, Disruption, Dissatisfaction, Dissension, Disunity, Divination, Dominatrix, Ego, Envy, Fault-Finding, Fierce Determination, Finger Pointing, Greed, Haughtiness, I Am More Important, I Am The Best, I Go First, I Have The Last Word, I Know Better, I Win, I'm Better Than You, Inconsiderate, Interference, Intimidation, Jezebel, Judging,

Torahlessness, Lust of the Eyes, Lying, Malice, Manipulation, Nagging, Narcissism, Never Satisfied, Number One, Opposition, Overindulgence, People User, Possessiveness, Pride of Life, Rebellion, Resistance, Scheming, Seduction, Self, Self-Admiration, Self-Approval, Self-Centered, Self-Concern, Self-Idolatry, Self-Importance, Self-Interest, Selfishness, Self-Obsessed, Self-Righteousness, Self-Seeker, Separation, Slander, Spiritual Blindness, Spite, Strife, Stubbornness, Superiority, Taker not Giver, Unbelief, Vanity and Willfulness

Leviathan, King of the Children of Pride: *Spirits:* **(Job 41, 104:16, Isa. 27:1)** Led by Logic instead of Yahovah, Carnal Justification, Hinder Spiritual Growth, Disturbs Concentration In Torah Study, Hinders Spiritual Concentration In Prayer, Weariness In Worship, Spiritual Sleepiness, Blocks Mind from Truth, Pride, Mourning, Spiritual Darkness, Arrogance, Spiritual Pride, Ego, Rationalization, Distraction, Brooding, Melancholy, Depression, Gloominess, Mental Dejection, Irascibility, Spiritual Darkness, Ego

Markai, Markiah: Markai/Markiah Blocks Spiritual Understanding and Causes Spiritual Blindness.

Matriarchal Witchcraft: *Spirits:* Fear, Stress, Anxiety, Abandonment, Loss of Patriarchal Nurturing, Lack of Proper Nurturing, Hate, Hate of Authority Figures, Distrust Toward Others, Performance, Accusation, Drivenness, Scattered, Rage, Anger and Bitterness

Matriarchal: The Matriarchal Hierarchy is due to the absence of righteous men taking their Proper Position In the Spirit or the Absence of Men Physically. This include women who take the head of their homes. It is due to Absent Fathers, Improper Family Structure, Improper Male and Female Relationships, Improper Alignment, etc.

Mind Idolatry: *Spirits:* Pride, Intellectualism Rationalization and Ego

Morondo: Morondo blocks the Reading Of Torah and Blocks Spiritual Light.

Murder: *Spirits:* Unloving Spirit and Spirit of Death Murder or Suicide is the final plunge into the Bitterness Kingdom.

Occult: *Spirits:* Potions, Necromancy, Idolatry, White Magick, Black Magick, Sorcery, Fortune Telling, Tarot Wizardry, Witchcraft, Omens, Charms, Tokens Enchantment, Divination, Necromancy, Star Gazing Astrology, Soothsaying, Prognostication, Incense, Dream Books, Numerology, Candle Magick, Dreams, Incantation Superstition, Occult, Herbal Medicine, Mediumship, Kinship Rituals, Royal Rituals, Ancestral Intervention Reincarnation, etc.

Orion: Orion teaches us to compromise of the WORD o Yahovah/Torah, teaches us to seek after and cling to Counterfeit Gifts, gives us False Peace and Religious Piety.

Perfectionism: *Spirits:* Pride, Vanity, Frustration Irritability, Intolerance, Anger, Criticism and Schizophrenia

Pharmaceuticals: The Family of Pharmaceuticals teaches us to use or take anything and everything

Medical/Potions/ Cures to take our trust away from Yahovah. All Pharmaceuticals are Pharmakeia, including Herbal Medicine, Naturopathy, etc.

Phobias – Agoraphobia: This is caused by the Fear of having Severe Anxiety or Panic Attack in a place or situation where escape may be difficult or embarrassing. Starts about age 29.

Prince Charming: *Spirits:* Intellectual, Philosophical, Religious Spirits, False Gifts and Veneer of Spirituality

Rage and Anger: *Spirits:* Bitterness (against a Parent, Guardian, Male Figure, Spouse, etc.), Abuse, Abandonment, Rejection, Not receiving Love and Lack of Nurturing. Part of the Bitterness Kingdom.

Rahab: *Spirits:* Dragon and Pride (Isa. 51:9-10)

Rejection: *Spirits:* Bitterness, Unforgiveness, Hate, Retaliation, Resentment, Anger, Wrath, Violence, Murder, Fear, Bondage, Accusation, Recorder, Abuse, Slander, Self-Bitterness, Self-Unforgiveness, Self-Hate, Self-Resentment, Self-Retaliation, Self-Anger/Self-Wrath, Self-Violence and Self-Murder (Suicide)

Religion: *Spirits:* False Doctrine, Abuse Of Scripture, False Prophesy, Wealth Or Prosperity, Spiritual Status, False Prestige, Preacher's Whoop, Smooth Talker, Power Of Persuasion, Domination, Manipulation, Control, Charmer, Spiritual Ambition, Lack Of Accountability, Compromise, Cover-Up, Superiority, Verbal Abuse, Physical Abuse, Spiritual Weakness, Vain Arguments, Profane Fictions, Abuse Of Titles, Silly Myths, Irreverent Babble, Godless

Chatter, Demonic Intercessory Prayers, Rastafarianism, Village Shrine Rituals, False Worship, Religious Frenzy, Open Relationship With The Dead, Orisa Worship (Yoruba), Voodoo (Vodun), Ancestor Reverence, Ancestor Worship, Religion, Piousness, Magick, False Healing, Spiritualism, Witchcraft, Nature Worship, Incense Burning, Psychic Prayers, Spirit Possession, Idolatry, Islam, Church Splits, etc.

Remus, Remur: Remus or Remur causes Sleep In Spiritual Environment

Resentment: *Spirits:* Unloving Spirit and Spirit of Death. Part of the Bitterness Kingdom.

Reserpcarian,   Rucipacerian: Reserpcarian   or Rucipacerian is a controlling Spirit that Blocks Spirit and Free Will.

Self-Anger/Self-Wrath: *Spirits:* Unloving Spirit and Spirit of Death. Part of the Self-Bitterness Kingdom.

Self-Bitterness Kingdom: *Spirits:* Self-Unforgiveness, Self-Resentment, Self-Retaliation, Self-Anger, Self-Wrath, Self-Hate, Self- Violence and Self-Murder (Suicide)

Self-Hatred: *Spirits:* Unloving Spirit and Spirit of Death. Part of the Self-Bitterness Kingdom.

Self-Murder: *Spirits:* Unloving Spirit and Spirit of Death. Part of the Self-Bitterness Kingdom (with words or suicide).

Self-Pity: This is a self-Idolatry spirit that puts Self above Yahovah and others. It ties one to all Past Hurts, Failures and Disappointments causing us to become Self-Consumed.

Self-Resentment: *Spirits:* Unloving Spirit and Spirit of Death. Part of the Self-Bitterness Kingdom.

Self-Retaliation: *Spirits:* Unloving Spirit and Spirit of Death. Part of the Self-Bitterness Kingdom.

Self-Unforgiveness: *Spirits:* Unloving Spirit and Spirit of Death. Part of the Self-Bitterness Kingdom.

Self-Violence: *Spirits:* Unloving Spirit and Spirit of Death. Part of the Self-Bitterness Kingdom.

Semiramus Spirit: Abortion, Accusation, Adita, Adultery, Aggression, Aida, Aida-Odeo, Altercation, Anahita, Anal Sex, Anat, Anti-Submissiveness, Aphrodite, Archia, Ardvi, Arguing, Argumentative, Ariadne, Arianhod, Arkh, Arrogance, Artemis, Ascendancy, Ashera, Asherim, Ashtaroth, Ash-Toret, Ashtoreth, Ash-Turit, Asmodeus, Assert, Astarte, Asterie, Astoreth Of The Sidonians, Astrea, Astrology, Atargatis, Athena, Athena, Athene, Athirat, Attention Seeking, Authoritarian, Belittlement Of Sons (or Daughters), Belittling, Beltis, Black Magic, Blessed Virgin Mary, Artemis, Burning Of Dedicated Candles, Burning Passion, Censure, Ceres, Cerridwen, Channeling, Charismatic Witchcraft, Charms, Child Abuse, Child Molestation, Child Murderer, Child Neglect, Child Pornography, Clash, Condemnation, Conflict, Confusion, Conjurations, Conniving, Contention, Lying, Control, Counterfeit Spiritual Gifts, Covetousness, Crystal Ball,

Crystals, Curses, Cybele, Dana, Deception, Defiance, Defilement, Delilah, Delusion, Demeter, Destruction Of Sons (or Daughters), Destruction, Determined Maneuvers, Diana, Dione, Discord, Disobedience, Dissension, Disunity, Divination, Dominance, Driving, Ego, Enchantment, Enheduanna, Envy, Eros, Fantasy, Fear, Female Dominance, Fetishes, Fierce Determination, Finger Pointing, Fire Gazing, Fornication, Fortune Telling, Gaia, Goddess Of Justice, Goddess Of The Groves, Goddess Of Wisdom, Goddesses Of The Virgin Themis, Greed, Harlotry, Hathor, Hatred Of Sons (or Daughters), Hatred, Haughtiness, Headstrong, Hexes, Horoscopes, Humiliation Of Sons (or Daughters), I Have The Last Word, I Know Better, I Win, I'm Better Than You, Immaculately Conceived, Mother Of The Gods, Inability to Give or Receive Love, Inanna, Incantations, Incubus, Inordinate Affection, Intimidation, Ishtar, Diana Of The Romans, Isis, Ixmucane, Josephine, Kabala, Kali, Lawlessness, Lust, Lying, Manipulation, Medium, Melissa, Melitta, Melitza, Melusine, Mental Abuse, Mind Control, Minerva, Moon Goddess, Mother Of Cheating, Mother Of Lies, Mother Of The Gods, Murder, My Choices Are The Best, Mylitta, Narcissistic, Nashe The Mediatrix, Number One, Odeo, Opposition, Osmodeus, Overindulgence, Palmistry, Pasowee, Pendulum, People User, Perverse Spirit, Possessiveness, Potions, Prejudice, Pretension, Pride of Life, Pride, Prostitution, Psychic Powers, Psychological Abuse, Queen Of Heaven, Rape, Re-Anen, Rebellion, Resistance, Retaliation, Revenge, Rhea, Ruler, Sadism, Santeria, Sati, Satyrism, Scheming, Self, Self-Admiration, Self-Approval, Self-Centered, Self-Concern, Self-Defeating, Self-Idolatry, Self-Importance, Self-Interest, Selfishness, Self-Obsessed, Self-Righteousness, Self-Seeker,

Self-Sufficiency, Semiramis, Sensitive, Sensuality, Separation, Sexual Abuse, Sexual Enticement, Sexual Impurity, Sexual Incitement, Shakti, Shame, Shing-Moo, Slander, Sleepiness, Smut, Songi, Sorcery, Sorrow, Spiritual Blindness, St. Barbara, Strategy, Superiority, Sura, Taker not Giver, Talismans, Tara, The Perfect One, The Queen, The Witch, Themis, Treachery, Tyrannical, Ungodly Discipline, Upper Hand, Vanity, Venus, Vexes, Virgin Mary, Voodoo, What I Say Is The Way It Is, What I Think Is The Way It Is, Whip Hand, White Magic, Wicca, Willfulness, Witchcraft and Worldly Wisdom

Sex: *Spirits:* Rape, Causing to Birth Illegitimate Children, Causing Teen Pregnancy, Prostitution, Men Sharing same Sexual Partner, Women sharing same Sexual Partner, Low Morals, Lust, Barrenness, Spirit of Bastard, Flirting, Sexual Sin, Abortions, Pedophilia, Perversion, Homosexuality, Lesbianism, Seduction, Fornication, Abuse, Rape, Assault by Penis, Behemoth, Sexual Promiscuity, Adultery, Fornication, Incest, Sodomy, Pornography, Sex Toys, Oral Sex, Anal Sex, Bestiality, etc.

Sexual Immorality: *Spirits:* Adulterous Affairs, Pornography, Greed, Sexual Immorality, Spirit of Lust, Fornication, Anger and Rage

Shame: *Spirits:* Self-Bitterness, Self-Unforgiveness, Self-Resentment, Self-Retaliation, Self-Anger/Self-Wrath, Self-Hate, Self-Violence and Self-Murder

Slavery: *Spirits:* Slavery, Fear, Distrust, Envy, Murder, Control, Physical Abuse, Desperation, Mental Weakness, being Hunted, Being Chased, Lynching Spirit, Vigilant Spirit. etc.

Spirits Affecting the Body: *Spirits:* Blackouts, Hangovers Sleeplessness, Nervous Stomach, Nervousness, Headaches Physical Illness, Poor Eating Habits, Nervous Breakdown Cirrhosis, Hypoglycemia, Liver Disorders and Physical Illnesses

Spirits Affecting the Family: *Spirits:* Spiritual Disorder Religious Spirits, Spiritual Blindness, Rebellion against Yahovah, Rebellion against Torah, Spiritual Deafness, Child Abuse, Sexual Molestation of Children, Slow Destruction through Addiction, Dysfunctional, Destruction of the Family Priest, Jezebel, Ahab, Torahlessness (Lawlessness) Secretiveness, Defensiveness, Don't Trust, Pharisaism Legalism, Self-Righteousness, Hatred of Responsibility Don't Feel, Family Despair, Family Embarrassment, Family Hopelessness, Hatred of Children, Family Shame Selfishness, Perversion, Sadism and Masochism

Spirits Affecting the Mind: *Spirits:* Anxiety, Fear of Being Rejected, Mental Instability, Paranoia, Escapism, Fear of Failure, Mind Blanking, Resentment, Fear of Being Unwanted, Schizophrenia, Guilt, Insecurity, Self-Hatred Intimidation, Hopelessness, Hatred of Others, Inability to Give Love, Inability to Receive Love, Impairment of Judgment, Indecision, Shame, Condemnation, Depression Inability to Communicate, Slow Thinking, Worthlessness Despair, Sorrow, Emptiness, No Hope, Emotional Illness Jealousy, Insanity, Madness, Suffering, Loneliness, Despair Suicide, Death, Low Self-Esteem, Torment, Fears of all kinds, Blurred Mind, Confusion, Deep Hurt, Defeatism and Failure

Spirits Affecting the Personality: *Spirits:* Lack of Personality, Lack of Accountability, Wrong Attitudes, Inappropriate Behavior towards Others, Controlling Others, Emotional Immaturity, Contentiousness, Alibis, Distortion, blame, Losing Jobs, Excuses, Lying, Deception, Denial, Unreliability, Irresponsibility, Arrogance, Fantasy, Self-Centeredness, Materialism, Atheism, Self-Righteousness, Big I – Little You, Selfishness, Spiritual Blindness, Lack of Discipline, Hypocrisy, Exaggerated Self-Importance, Religious Spirits, I am Important – You are Not, Compulsiveness, Idleness, Foolishness, Poverty Mentality, Reckless Driving, Disorderliness, Laziness, Sluggishness, Forgetfulness, Slothfulness, Mischievousness, Wastefulness, Reckless Spending, Perfection, Ahab & Jezebel, Unwilling to Hear, Biting Like a Serpent, Caustic Verbal Abuse, Verbal Abuse, Matriarchal Witchcraft, Insubordination to Authority, Isolation, Deep Insecurity, Disrespect, Jeering, Sneering, Pouting, Negative Attention Getting, Physical Abuse, Explosive Temper, Rejection, Hindered Watchfulness, Putting Down Others, Childishness, Immature Thinking, Debilitating Putdown and Infantile Social Behavior

Spirits Who Hurt Others: *Spirits:* Cruelty, Destruction, Explosion, Hatred, Offense, Slander, Malice, Violence, Gossip, Temper Tantrums, Malice, Rage and Seething Anger

Strife: *Spirits:* Pride, Self-Righteousness, Judgmental, Critical, Bitterness, Jealousy, Offence, Distrust of God. The root of everything evil. Strife = Unrest

Vanity: *Spirits:* Belphegar, Belfagar, Apollyon, Scorpion, Fears, Absalom, Pride, Orion, Perfection and Schizophrenia

Violence: *Spirits:* Unloving Spirit, Spirit of Death and Part of the Bitterness Kingdom.

White Skin Kingdom: *Spirits:* Arrogance, Fear, Slavery, Oppression, Prejudice, Theft, Pain, Brutality, Betrayal, Fear, Shame, Bitterness, Hatred, Etc.

Witchcraft - Control: Witchcraft results from stubbornness to the Torah, the Word of Yahovah. It stems from creating one's own ideas, own kingdom and own words.

MORE BOOKS BY THE AUTHOR AND FURTHER TEACHING:

KINDLE BOOKS

Ask For The Ancient Paths Kindle Edition

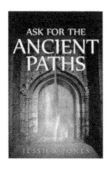

http://www.amazon.com/dp/B00COC81HQ

Soul Ties & Legal Ground Kindle Edition

http://www.amazon.com/dp/B00COEZHWQ

It's Time To Heal & Leave Your Rape Behind You Kindle Edition

http://www.amazon.com/dp/B00DZUQD30

Spiritual Roots of Disease Kindle Edition

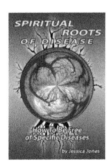

http://www.amazon.com/dp/B00FB061DO

Revealing the Bride of Y'shua Kindle Edition

Jessica Jones

https://www.amazon.com/dp/B00GMSZMKW

HARD COPY ONLY – PRINTED BOOKS
Exposing The Truth Paperback

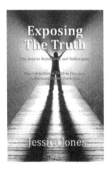

http://www.amazon.com/dp/0981454828

WEBSITE
www.askfortheancientpathsministry.com

RESOURCES FOR FOUNDATIONAL TEACHING

www.rootsofrestoration.com

www.199Ministries.org

www.aroodawakening.tv

Made in the USA
Las Vegas, NV
15 November 2022

59561683R00079